FOR ORGANS, PIANOS & ELECTRONIC KEYBOARDS

83

2nd Edition

Swingtime

T0066124

ISBN-13: 978-1-4234-1762-0
ISBN-10: 1-4234-1762-3

HAL•LEONARD®
CORPORATION
7777 W. BLUEMOUND RD. P.O. BOX 13819 MILWAUKEE, WI 53213

Visit Hal Leonard Online at
www.halleonard.com

CONTENTS

4 Ain't That a Kick in the Head

10 All of Me

7 Alright, Okay, You Win

15 Back in Your Own Backyard

18 The Best Is Yet to Come

20 Come Fly with Me

24 Do Nothin' Till You Hear from Me

26 The Frim Fram Sauce

28 Gone with the Wind

30 I'll Remember April

32 I'm Beginning to See the Light

34 I've Found a New Baby (I Found a New Baby)

36 In a Mellow Tone

38 The Lady Is a Tramp

12 Learnin' the Blues

40 Let's Fall in Love

42 Lullaby of the Leaves

44 Makin' Whoopee!

46 Pick Yourself Up

48 Same Old Saturday Night

50 Satin Doll

52 Sentimental Journey

54 Stompin' at the Savoy

56 Swinging on a Star

58 Tuxedo Junction

60 Witchcraft

62 You Came a Long Way from St. Louis

64 REGISTRATION GUIDE

Ain't That a Kick in the Head

Registration 2
Rhythm: Swing or Fox Trot

Words by Sammy Cahn
Music by James Van Heusen

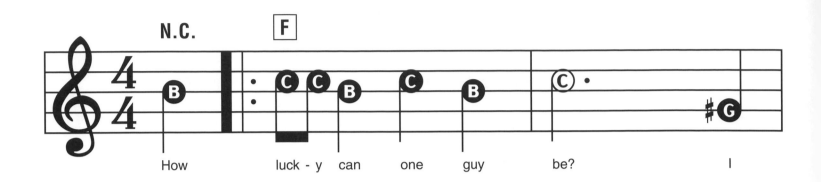

How luck - y can one guy be? I

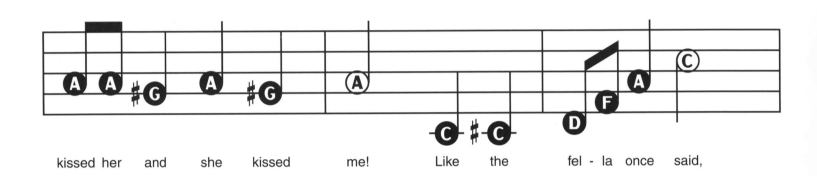

kissed her and she kissed me! Like the fel - la once said,

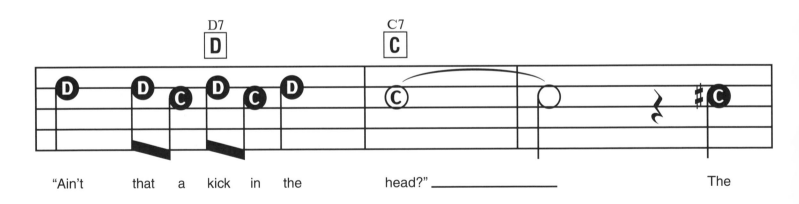

"Ain't that a kick in the head?" _____ The

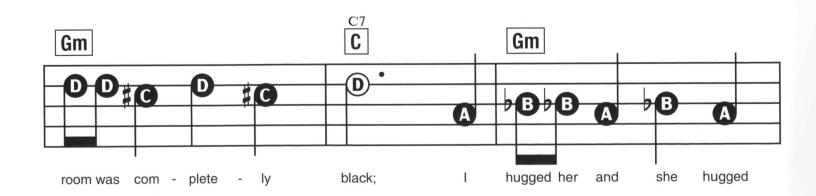

room was com - plete - ly black; I hugged her and she hugged

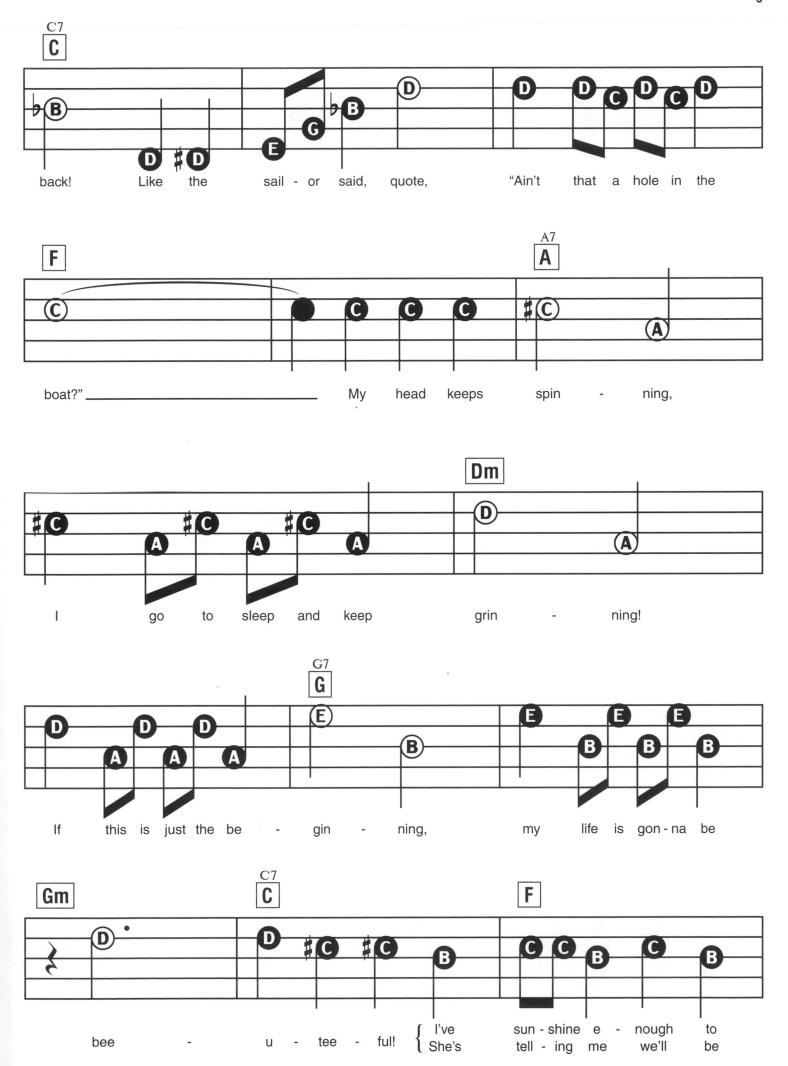

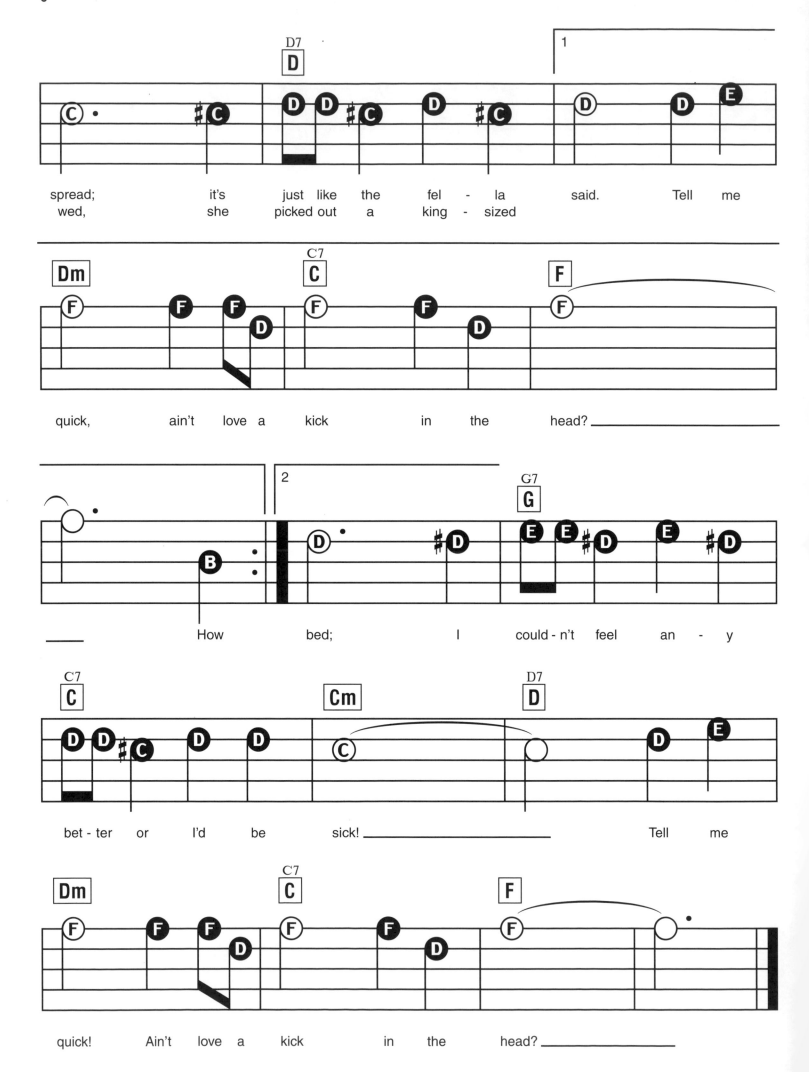

Alright, Okay, You Win

Registration 7
Rhythm: Swing

Words and Music by Sid Wyche
and Mayme Watts

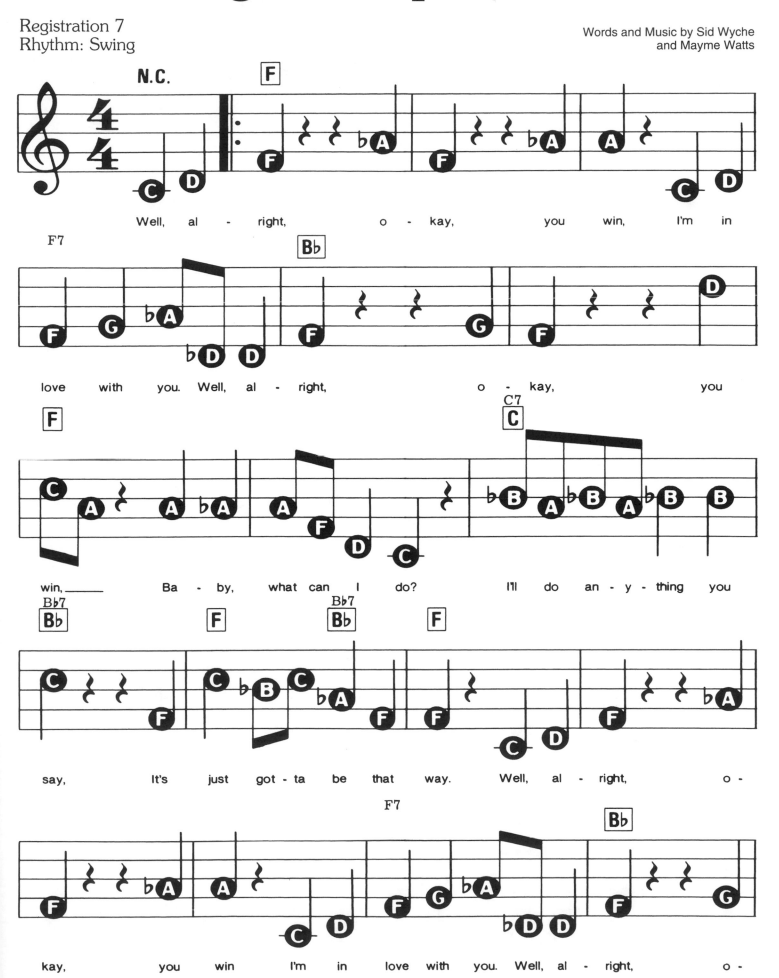

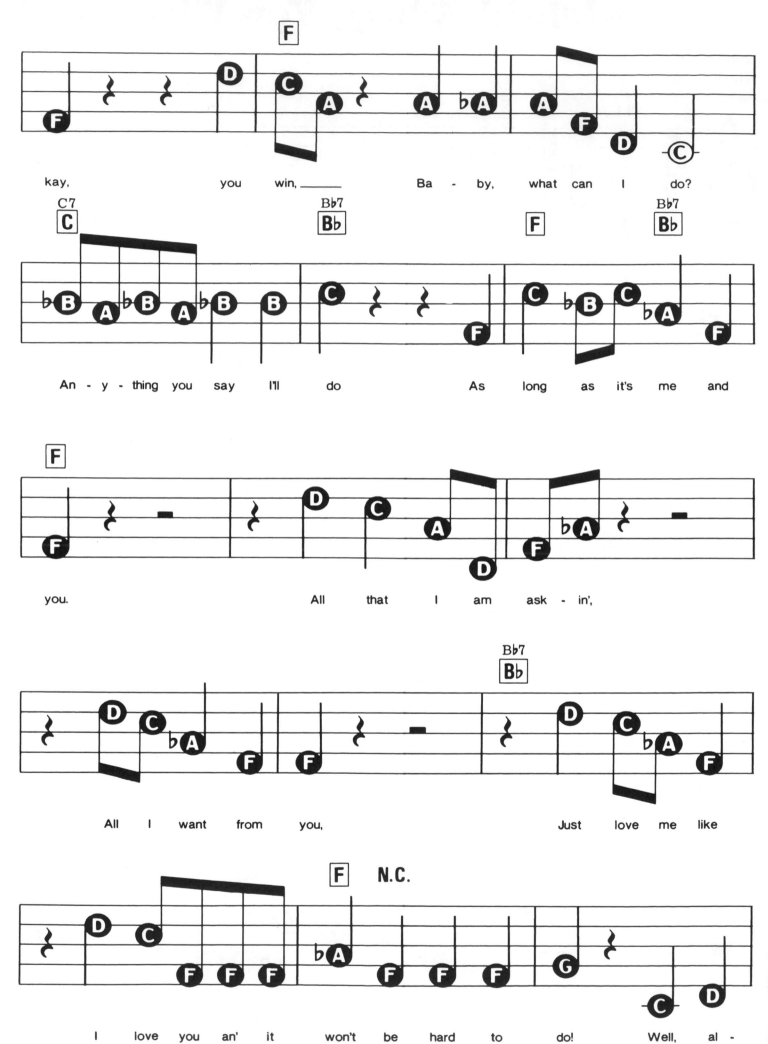

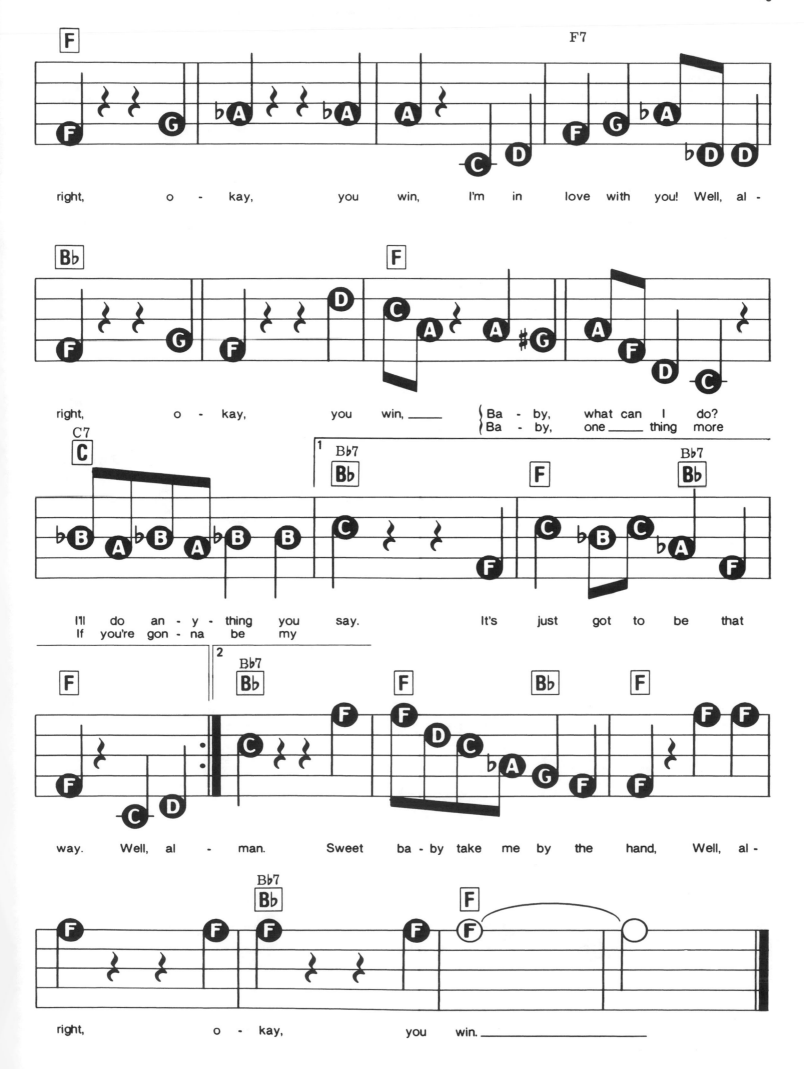

All of Me

Registration 4
Rhythm: Fox Trot or Swing

Words and Music by Seymour Simons
and Gerald Marks

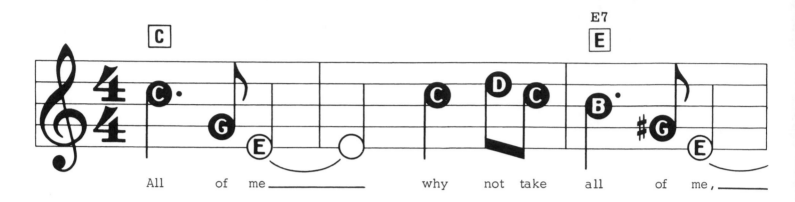

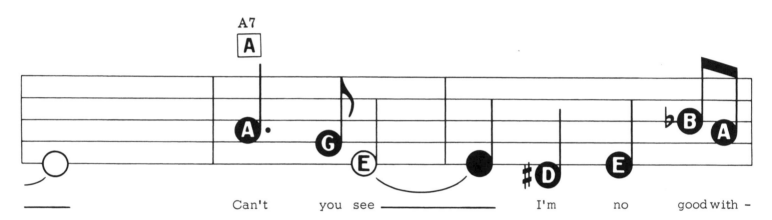

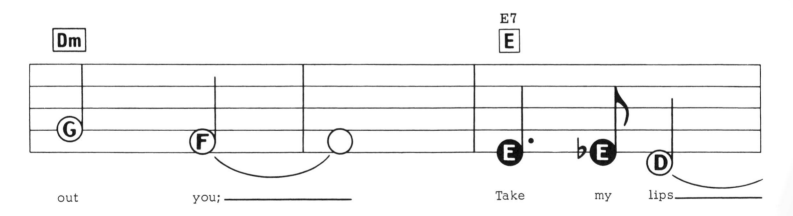

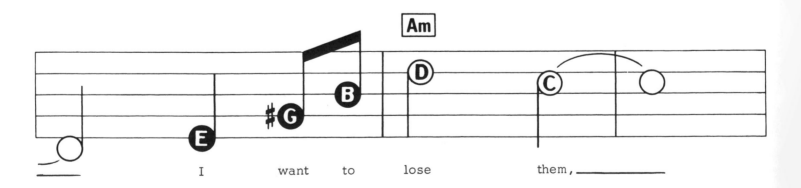

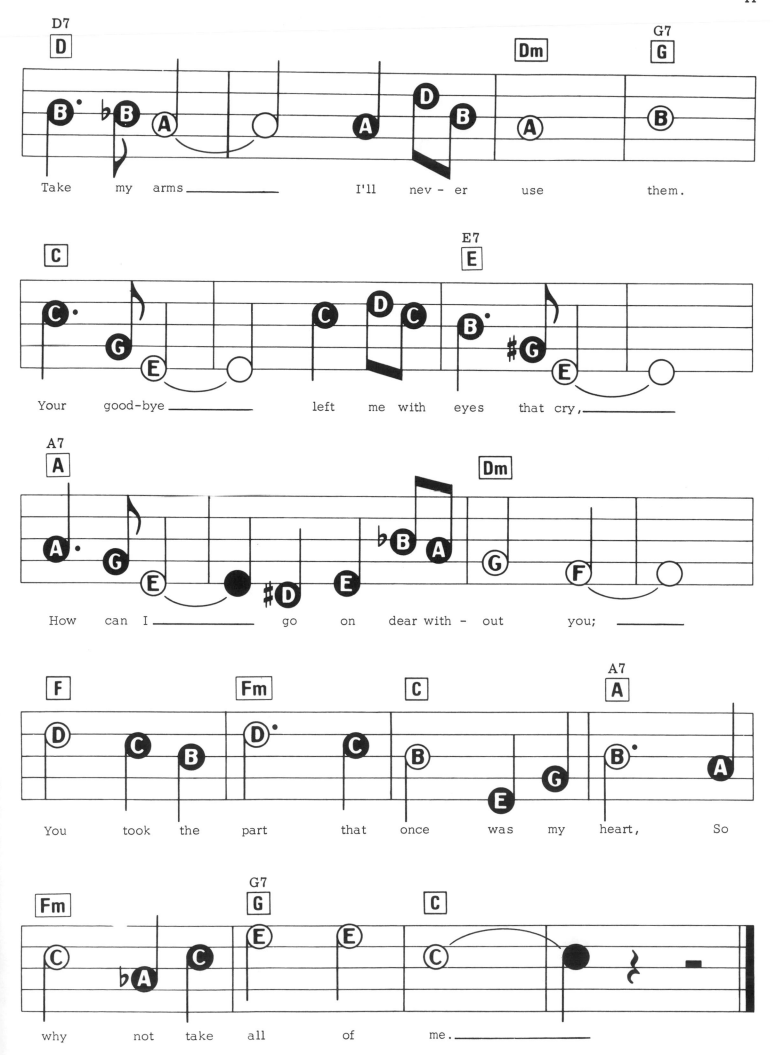

Learnin' the Blues

Registration 2
Rhythm: Swing

Words and Music by
Dolores "Vicki" Silvers

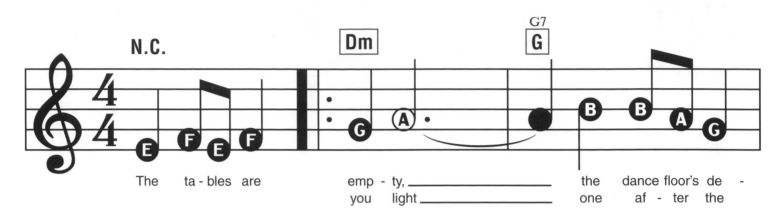

The ta - bles are emp - ty, _____ the dance floor's de -
you light _____ one af - ter the

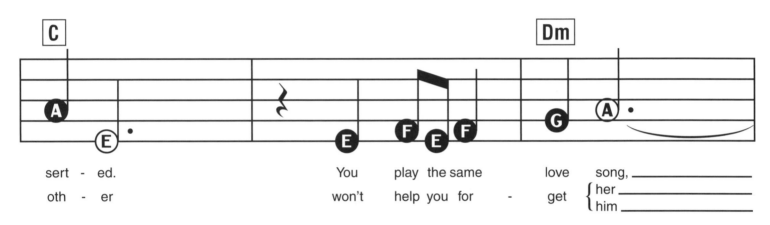

sert - ed. You play the same love song, _____
oth - er won't help you for - get { her _____
{ him _____

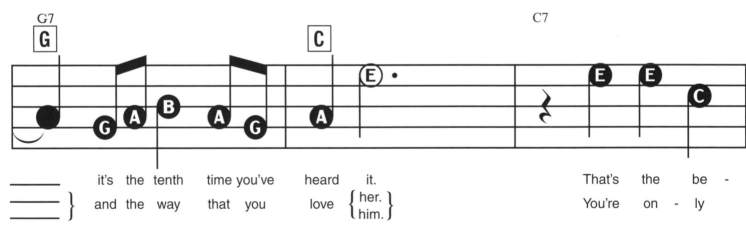

_____ it's the tenth time you've heard it. That's the be -
_____ } and the way that you love { her. } You're on - ly
{ him. }

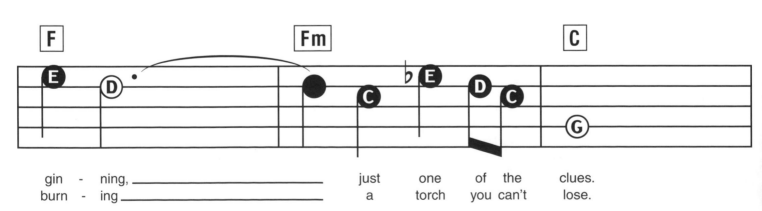

gin - ning, _____ just one of the clues.
burn - ing _____ a torch you can't lose.

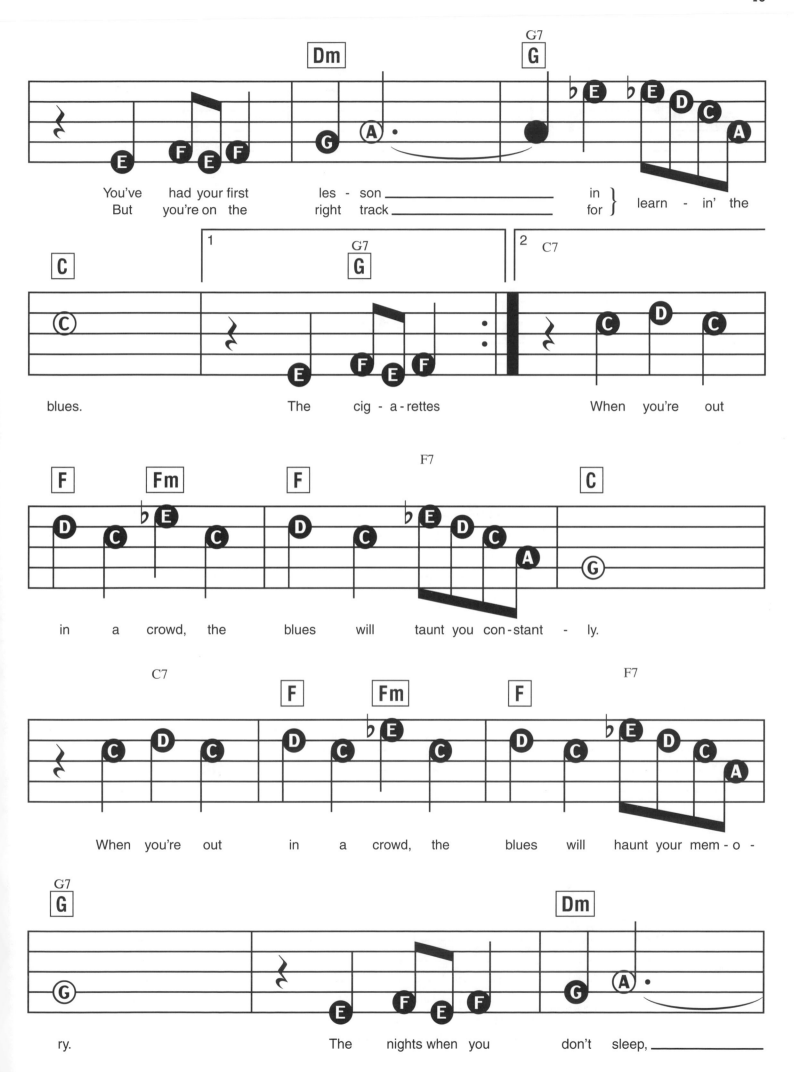

13

14

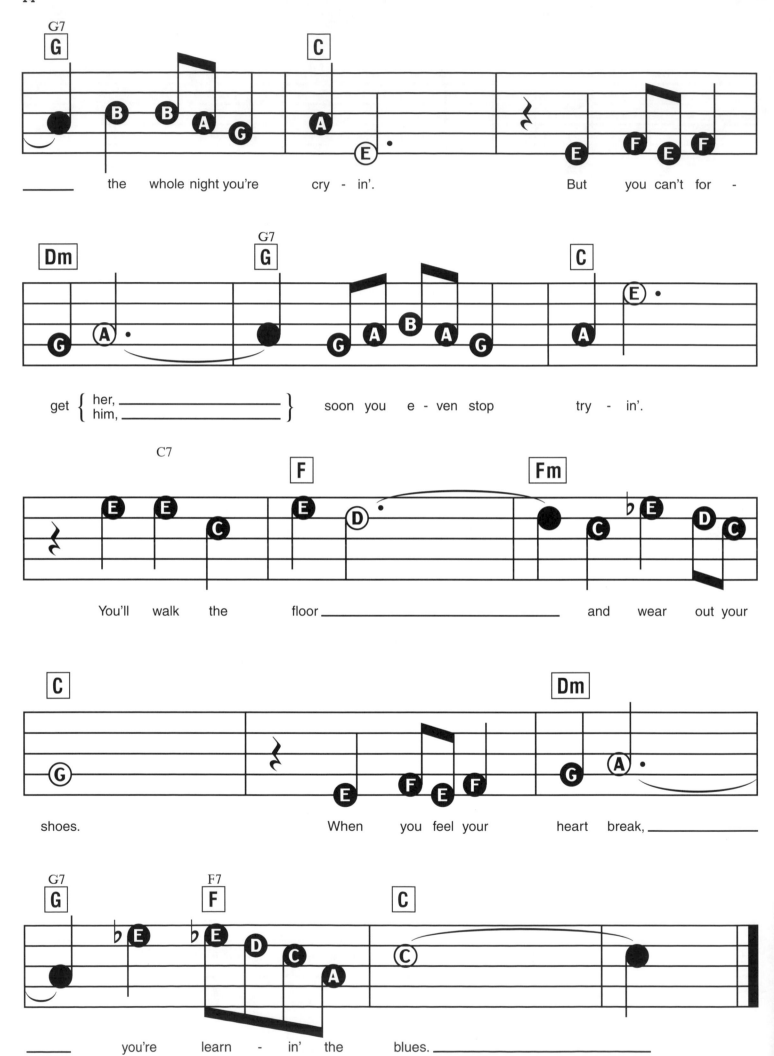

Back in Your Own Backyard

Registration 10
Rhythm: Swing

Words and Music by Al Jolson,
Billy Rose and Dave Dreyer

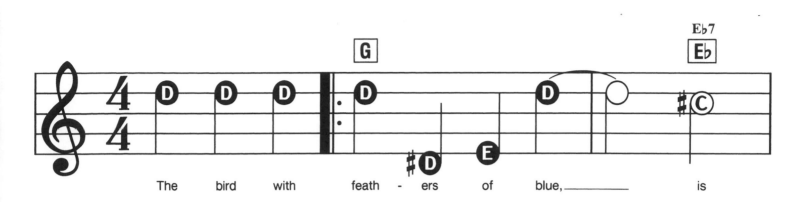

The bird with feath - ers of blue, _____ is

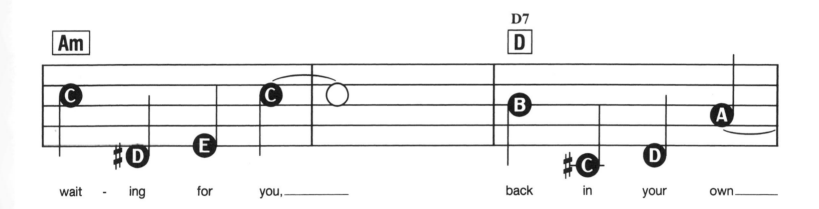

wait - ing for you, _____ back in your own _____

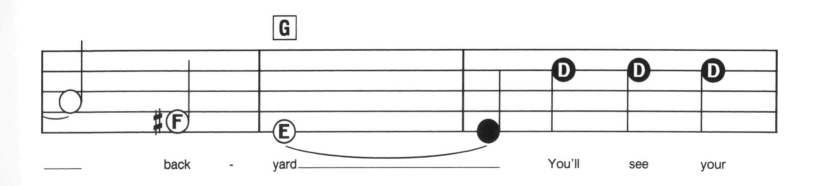

_____ back - yard _____ You'll see your

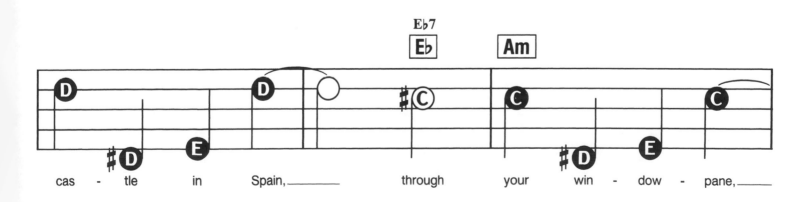

cas - tle in Spain, _____ through your win - dow - pane,

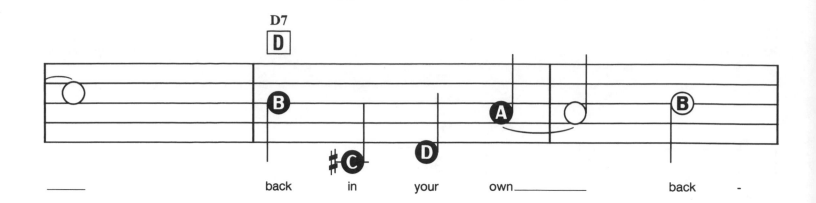

back in your own_____ back -

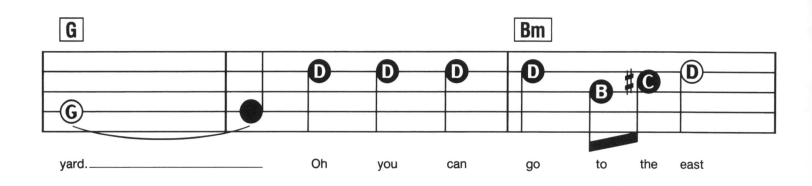

yard._____ Oh you can go to the east

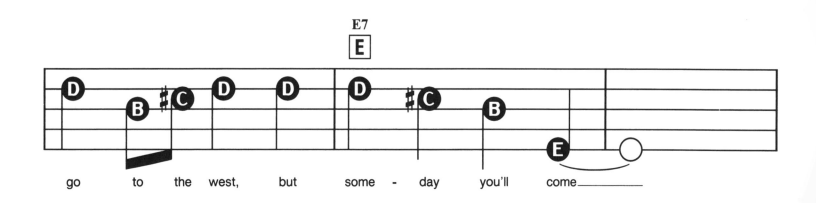

go to the west, but some - day you'll come____

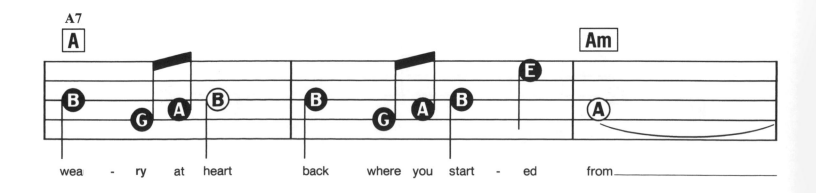

wea - ry at heart back where you start - ed from____

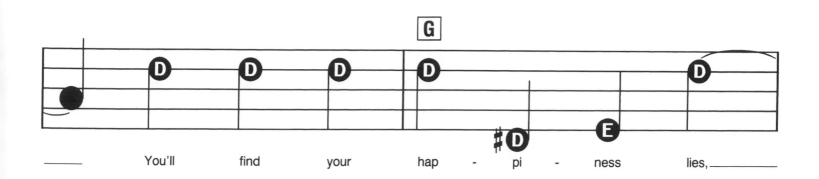

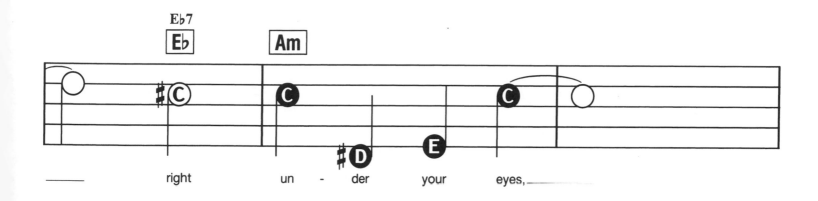

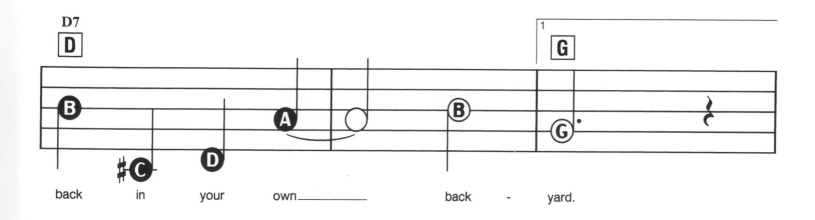

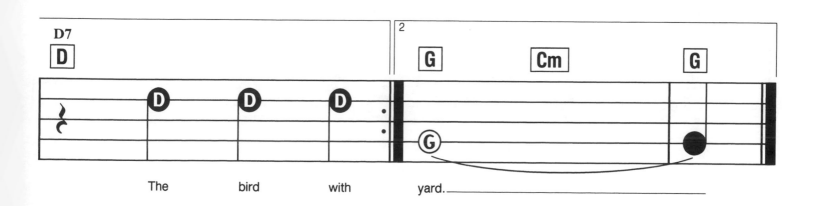

The Best Is Yet to Come

Registration 7
Rhythm: Swing

Music by Cy Coleman
Lyrics by Carolyn Leigh

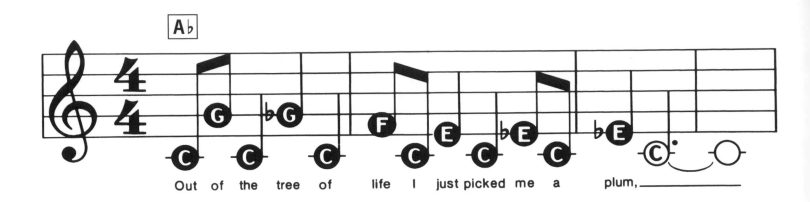

Out of the tree of life I just picked me a plum,_____

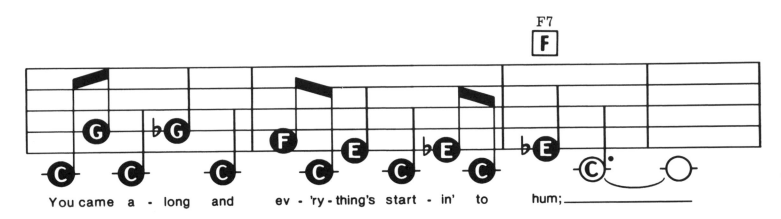

You came a - long and ev - 'ry - thing's start - in' to hum;_____

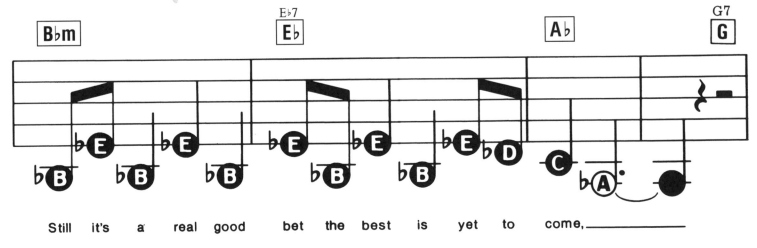

Still it's a real good bet the best is yet to come,_____

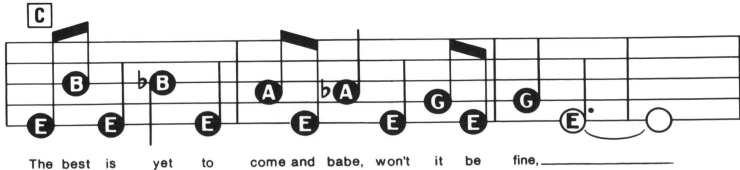

The best is yet to come and babe, won't it be fine,_____

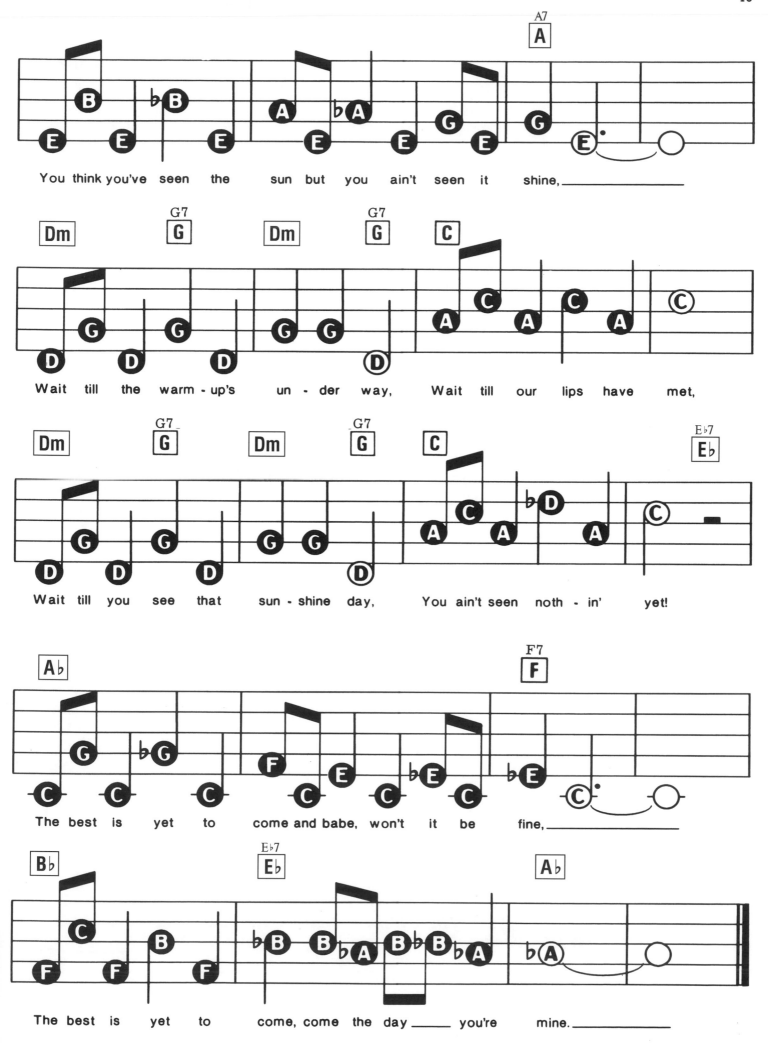

Come Fly with Me

Registration 4
Rhythm: Swing

Words by Sammy Cahn
Music by James Van Heusen

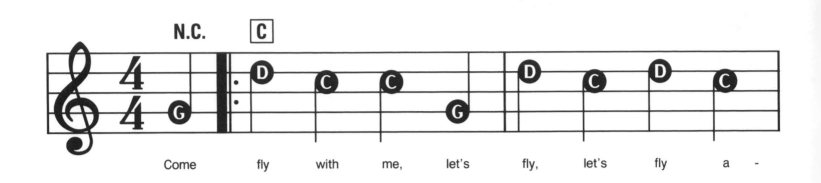

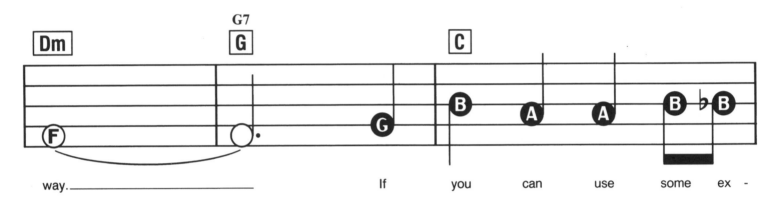

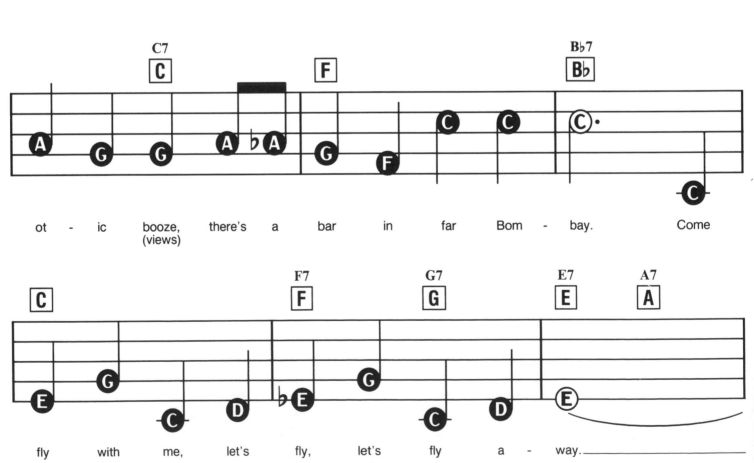

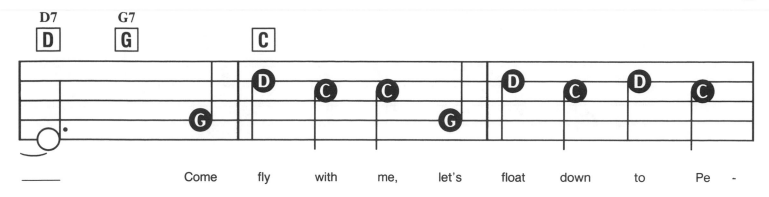

Come fly with me, let's float down to Pe -

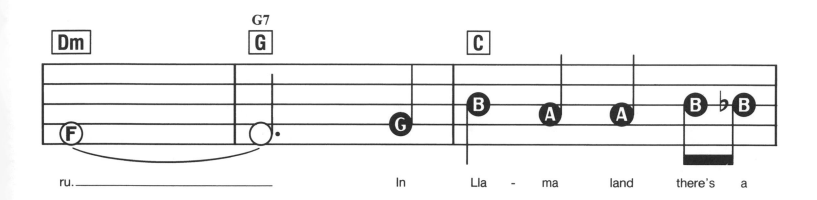

ru. In Lla - ma land there's a

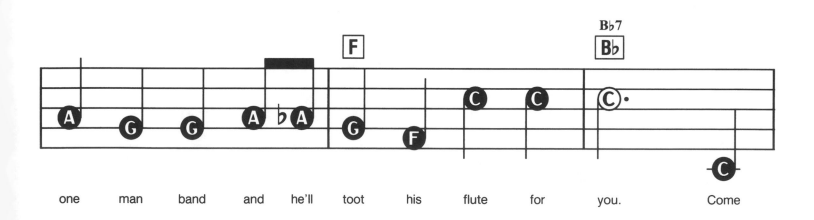

one man band and he'll toot his flute for you. Come

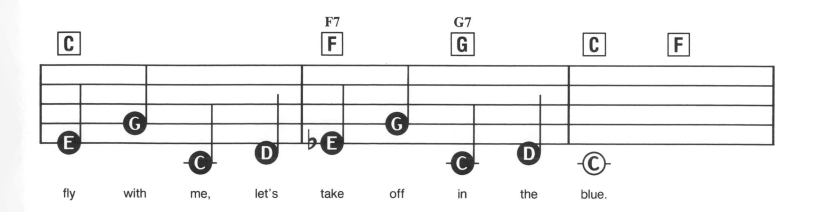

fly with me, let's take off in the blue.

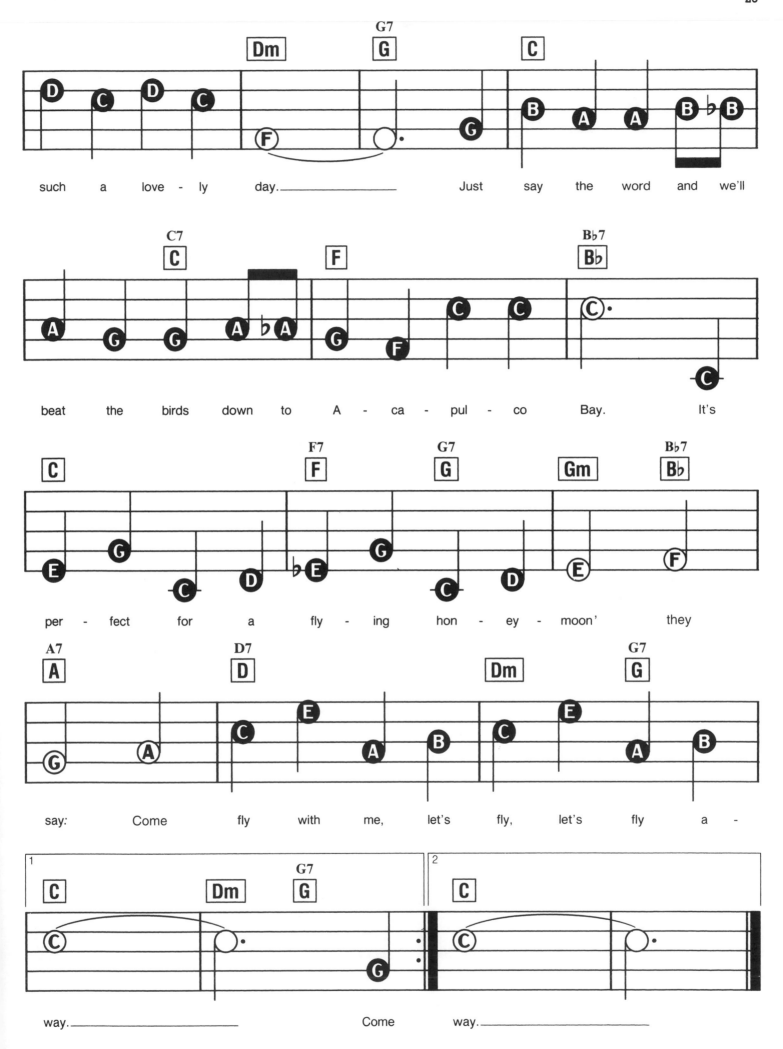

Do Nothin' Till You Hear from Me

Registration 7
Rhythm: Swing

Words and Music by Duke Ellington
and Bob Russell

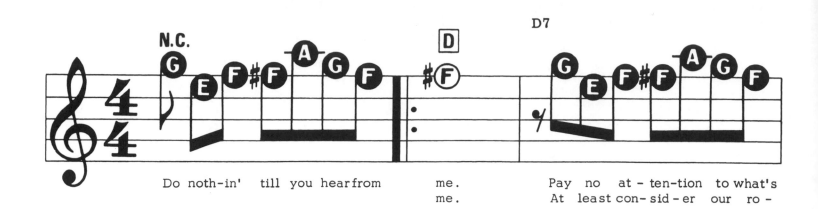

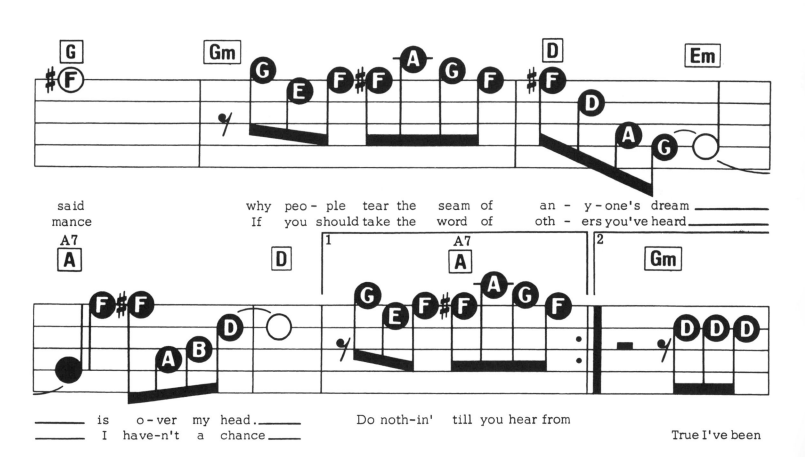

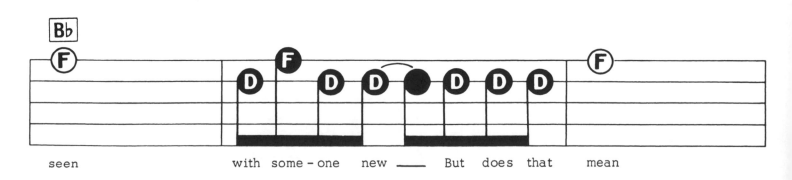

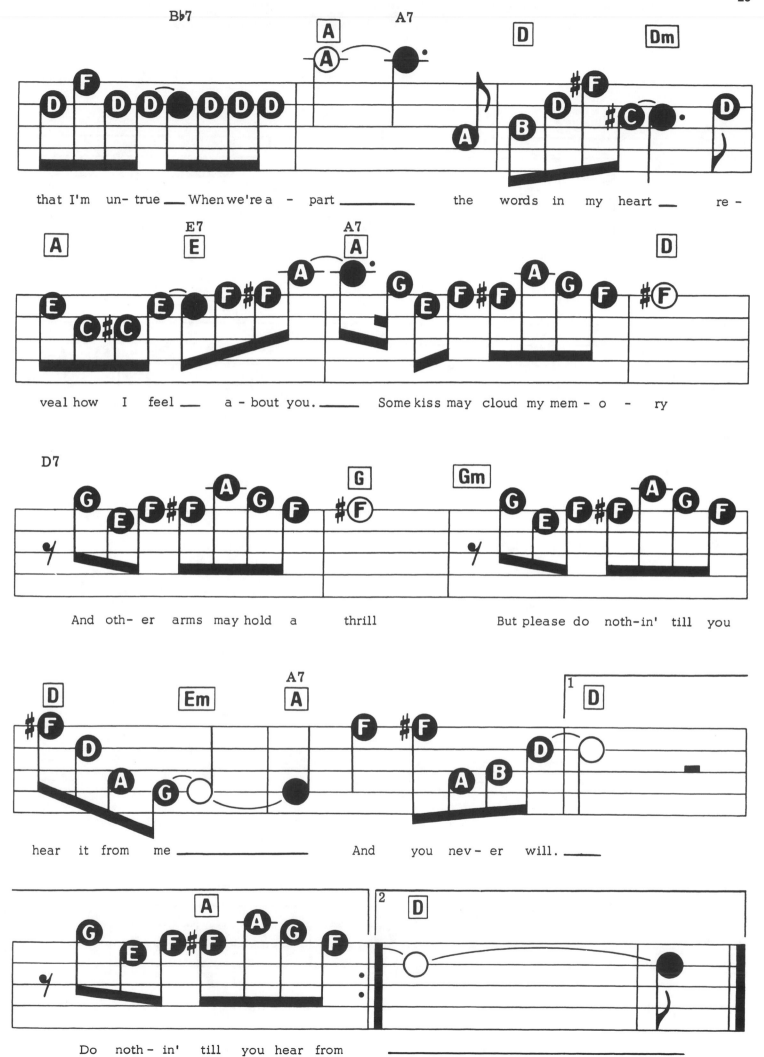

The Frim Fram Sauce

Registration 2
Rhythm: Swing

Words and Music by Joe Ricardel
and Redd Evans

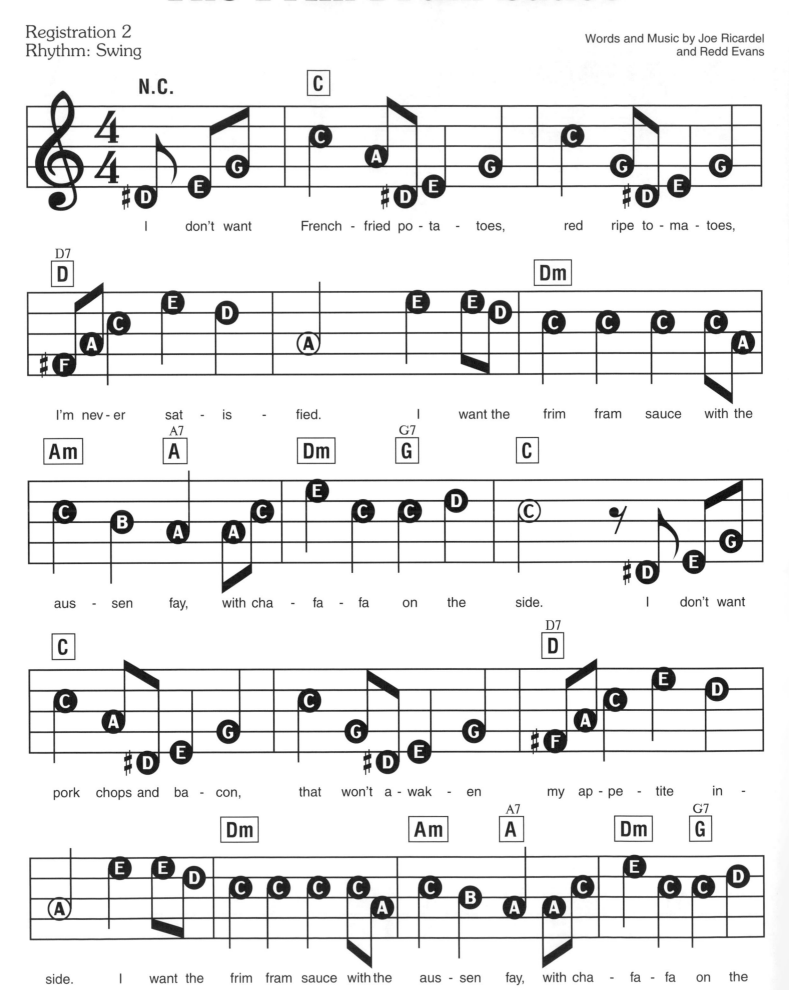

27

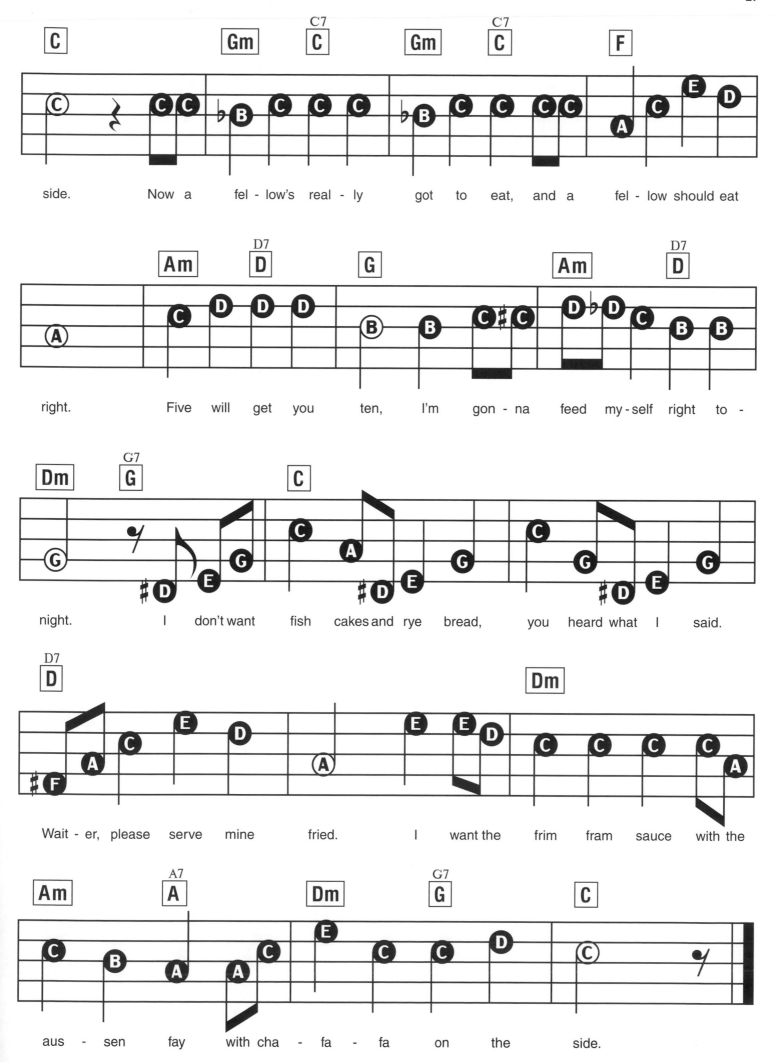

Gone with the Wind

Registration 2
Rhythm: Swing

Words and Music by Herb Magidson
and Allie Wrubel

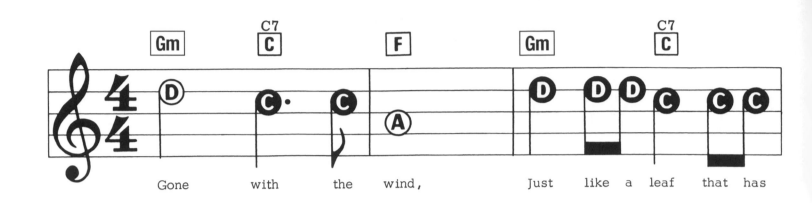

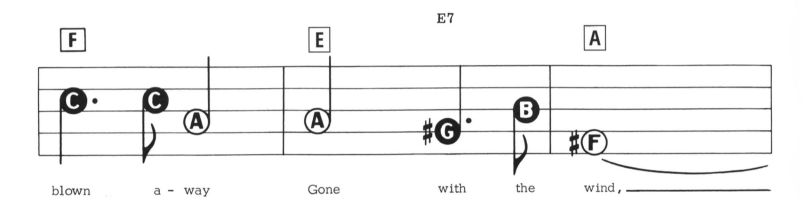

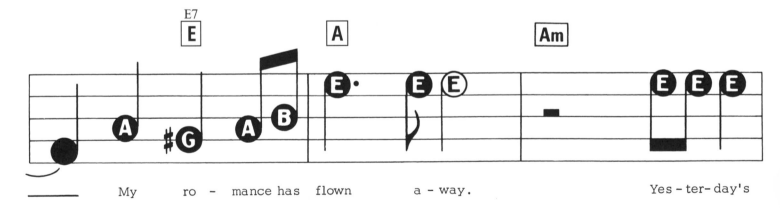

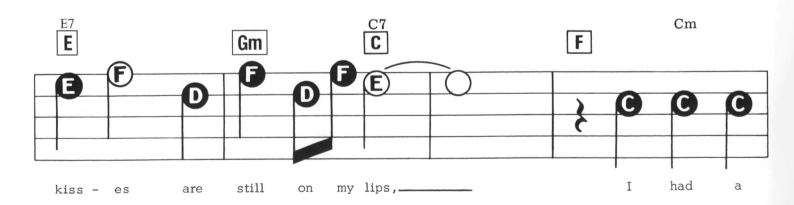

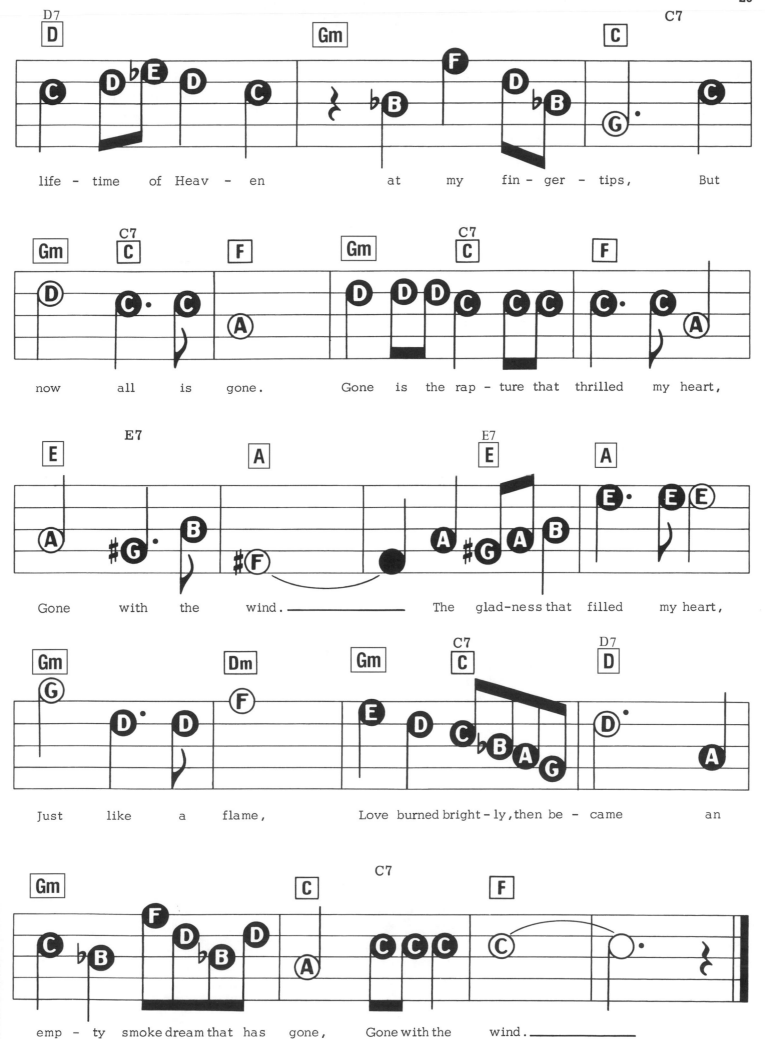

I'll Remember April

Registration 3
Rhythm: Swing

Words and Music by Pat Johnson,
Don Raye and Gene De Paul

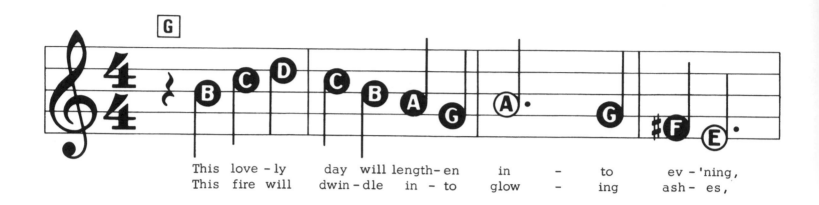

This love - ly day will length-en in - to ev -'ning,
This fire will dwin-dle in-to glow - ing ash - es,

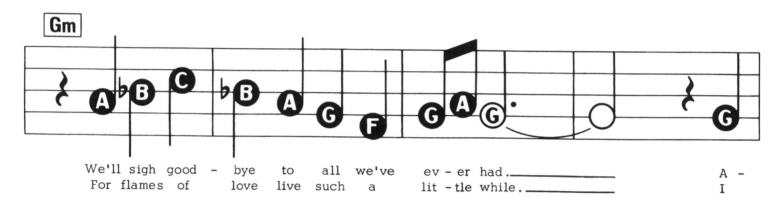

We'll sigh good - bye to all we've ev - er had._____ A -
For flames of love live such a lit - tle while._____ I

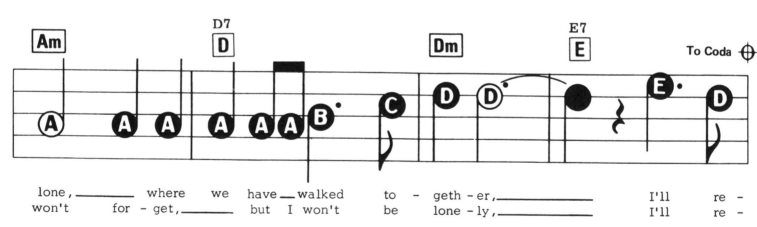

To Coda

lone,_____ where we have walked to - geth - er,_____ I'll re -
won't for - get,_____ but I won't be lone - ly,_____ I'll re -

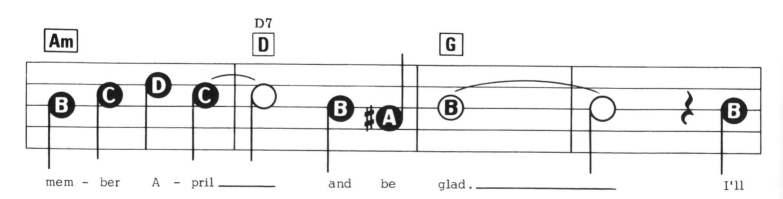

mem - ber A - pril _____ and be glad._____ I'll

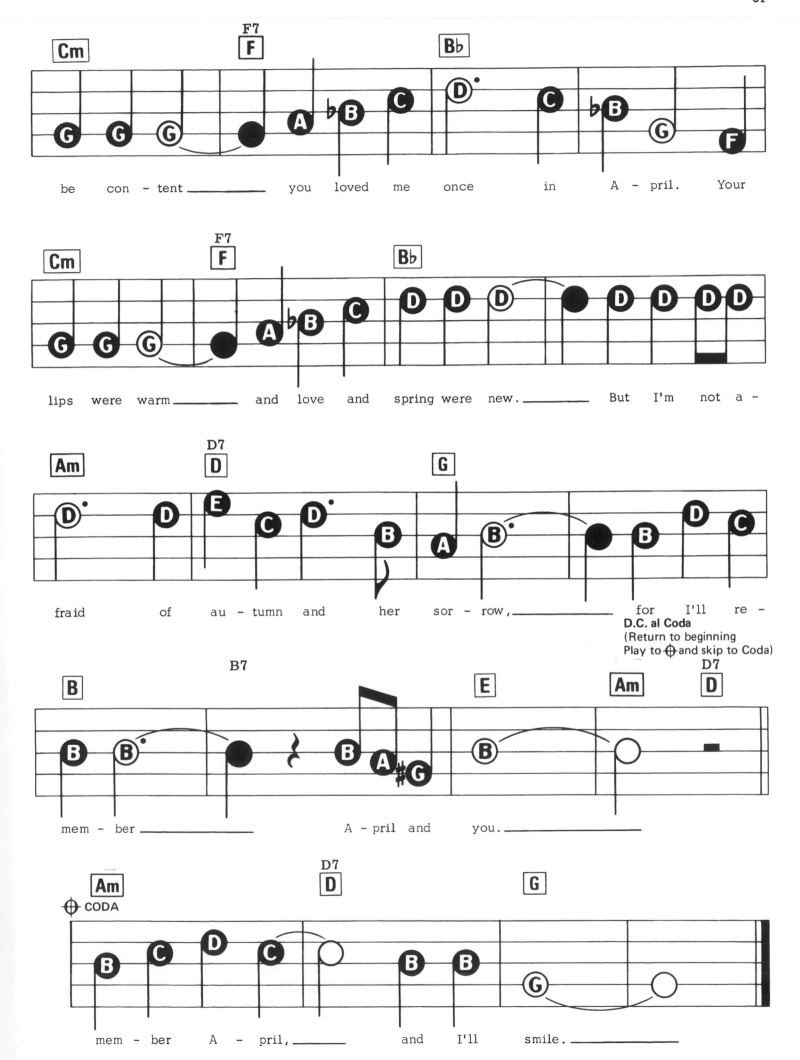

I'm Beginning to See the Light

Registration 4
Rhythm: Fox Trot or Swing

Words and Music by Don George,
Johnny Hodges, Duke Ellington and Harry James

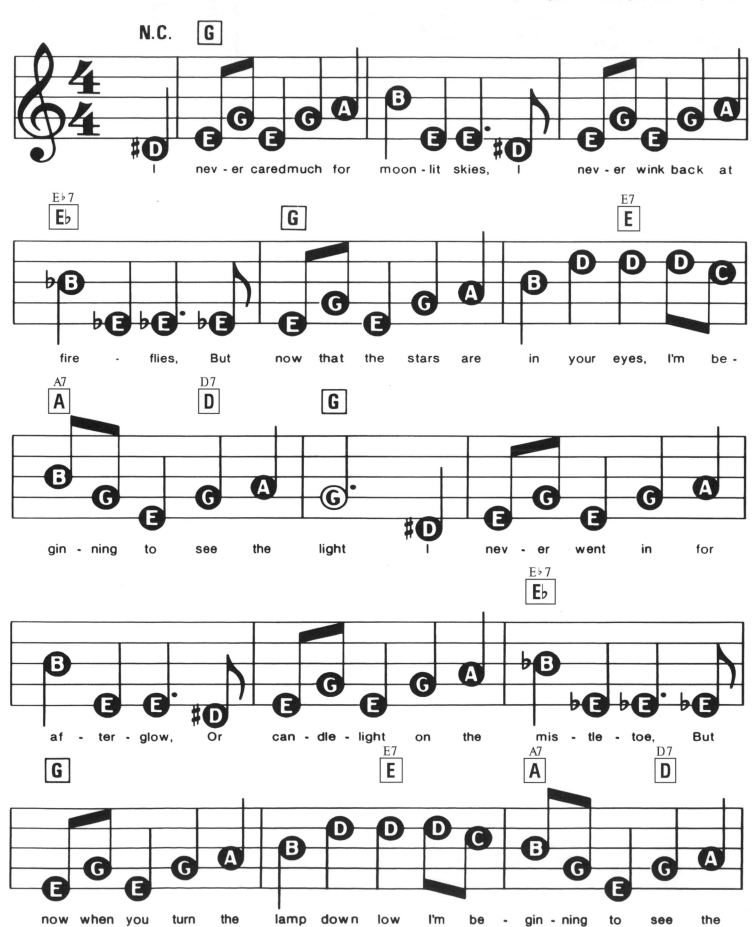

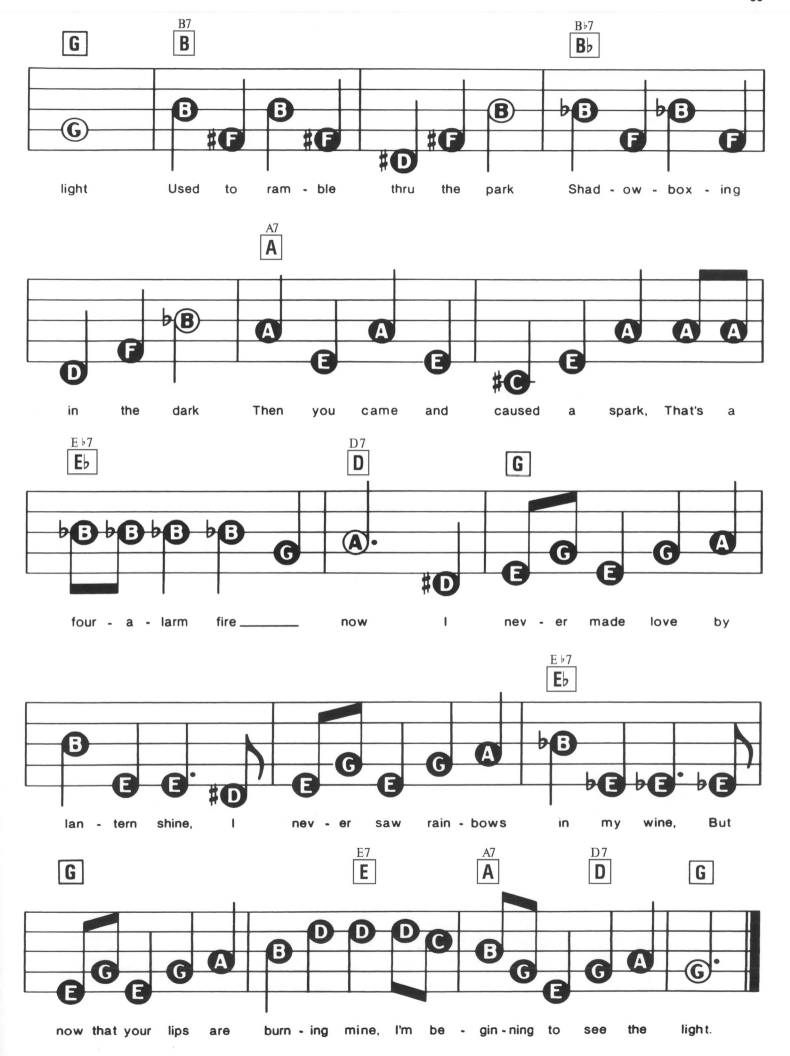

I've Found a New Baby
(I Found a New Baby)

Registration 8
Rhythm: Swing

Words and Music by Jack Palmer
and Spencer Williams

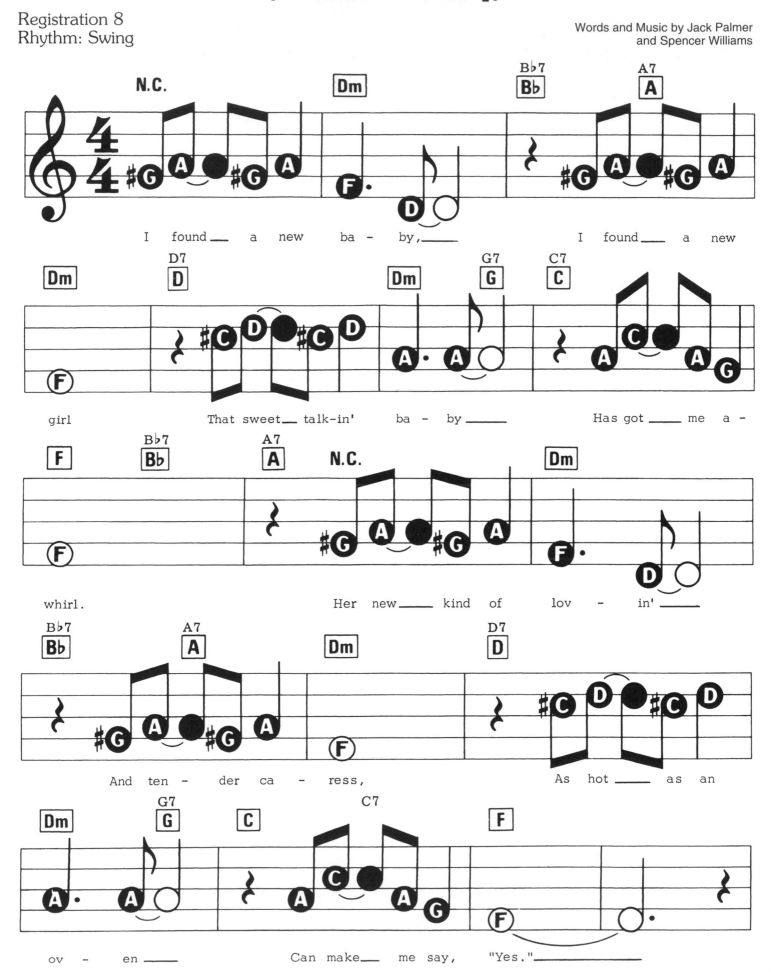

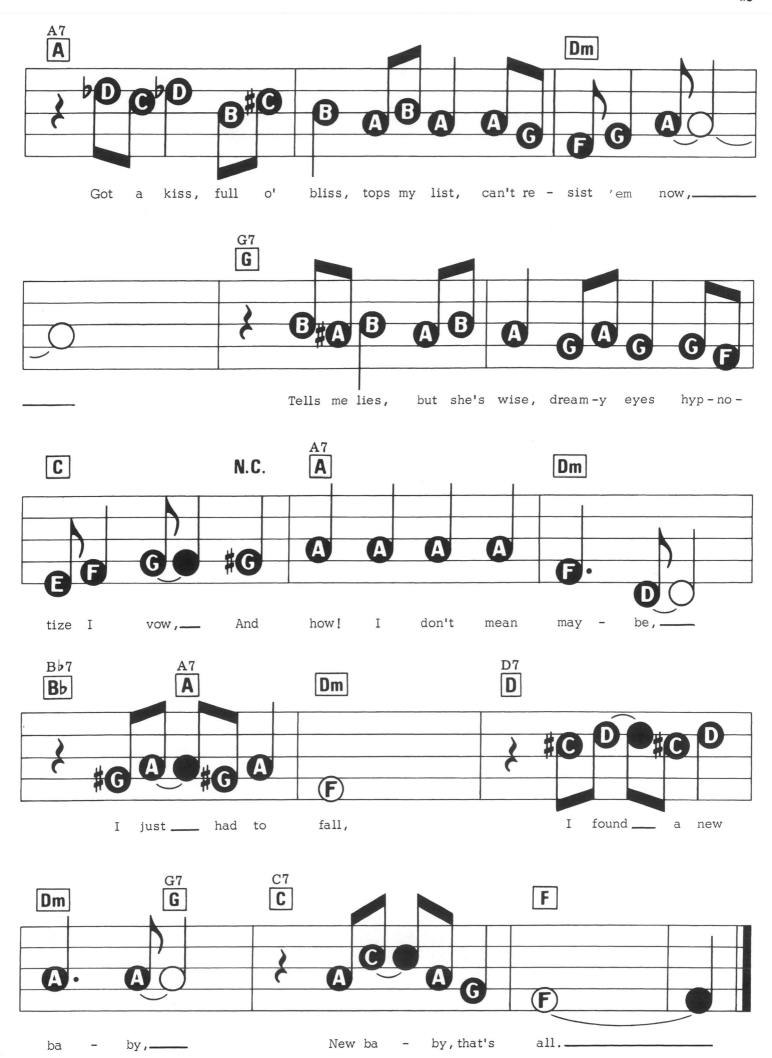

In a Mellow Tone

Registration 4
Rhythm: Swing or Fox Trot

Words by Milt Gabler
Music by Duke Ellington

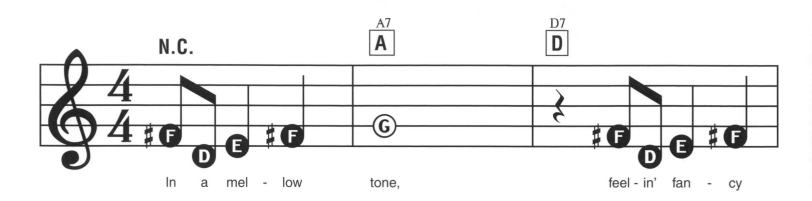

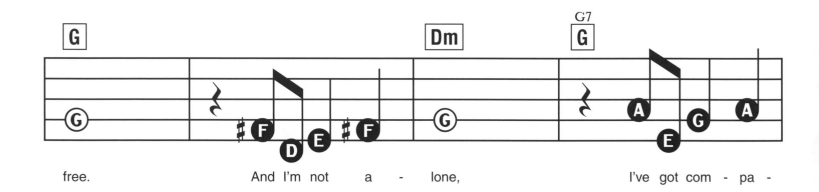

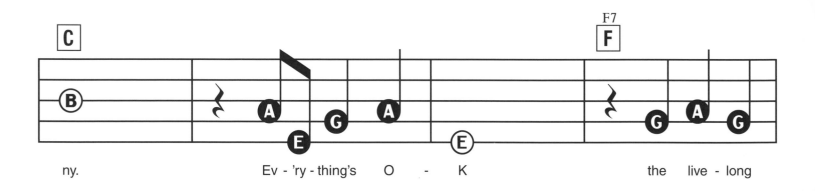

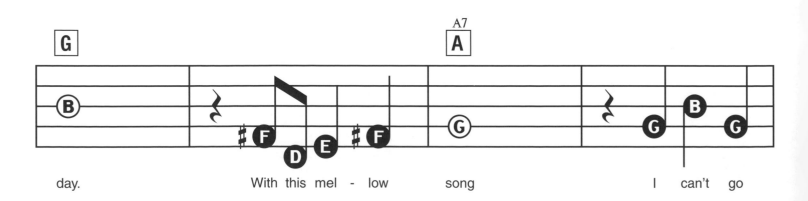

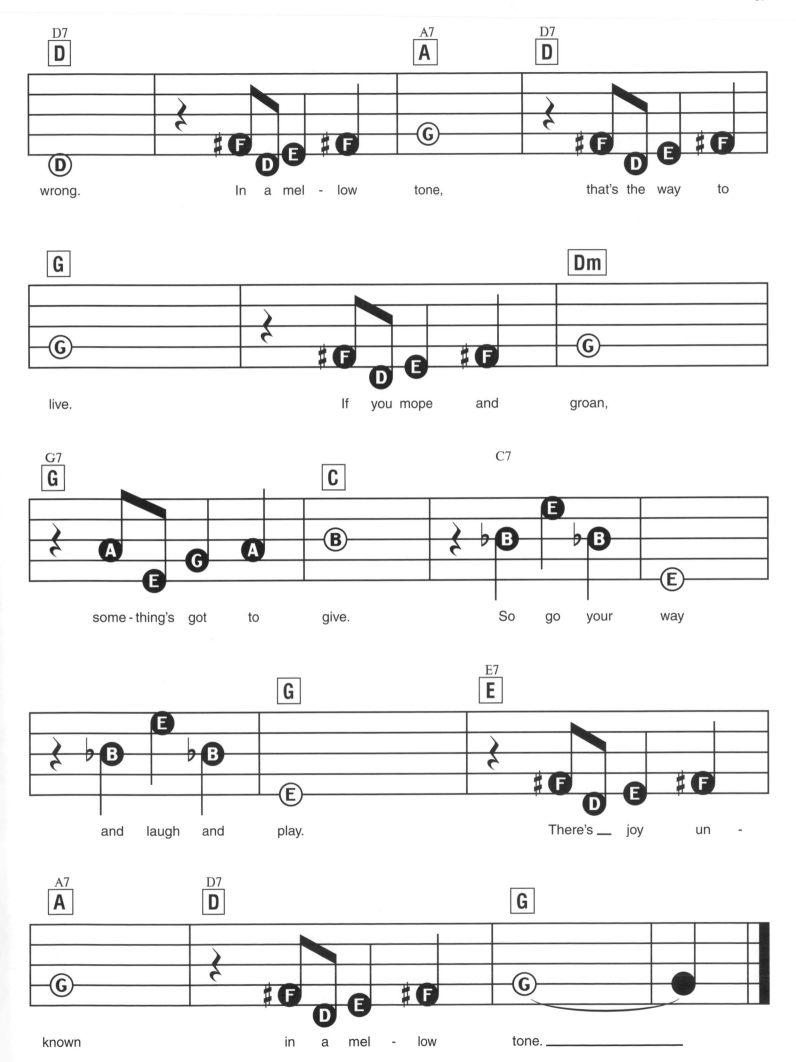

The Lady Is a Tramp
from BABES IN ARMS
from WORDS AND MUSIC

Registration 7
Rhythm: Fox Trot or Swing

Words by Lorenz Hart
Music by Richard Rodgers

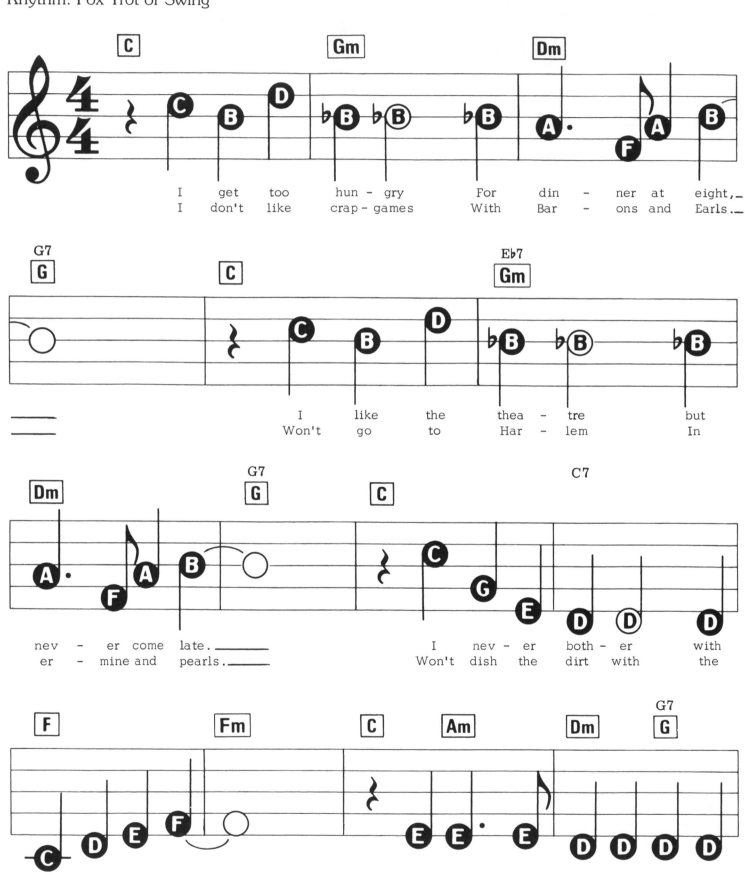

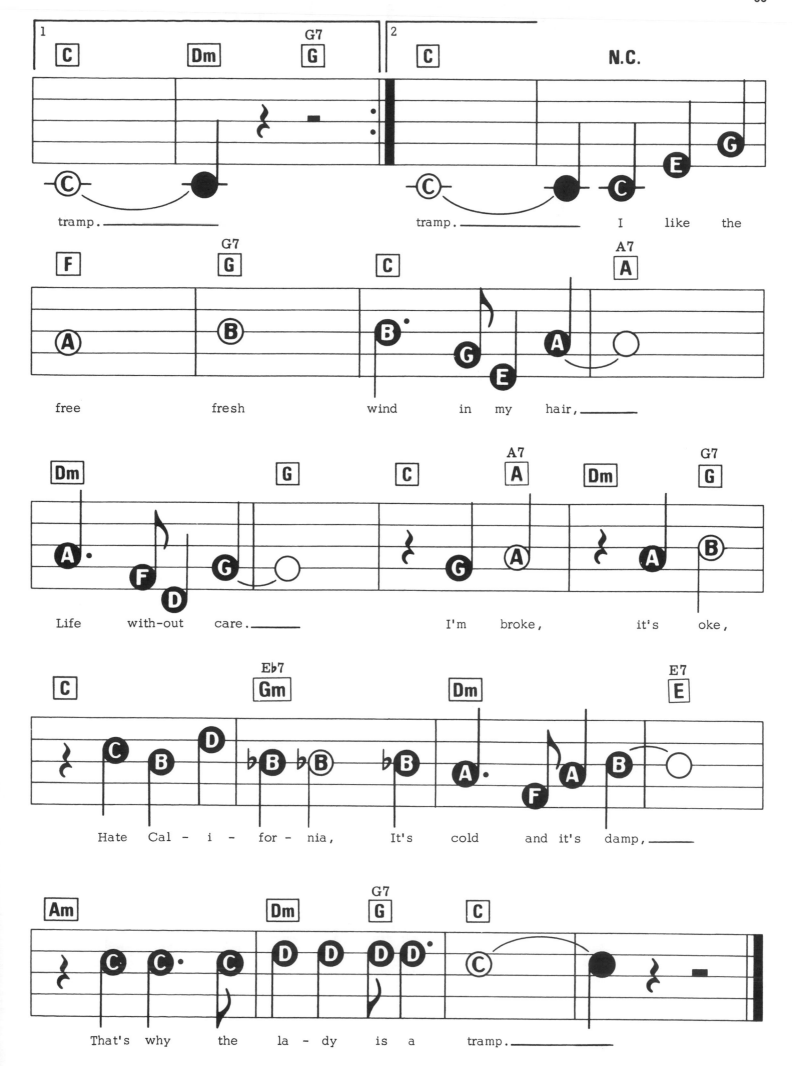

Let's Fall in Love

Registration 9
Rhythm: Fox Trot or Swing

Words by Ted Koehler
Music by Harold Arlen

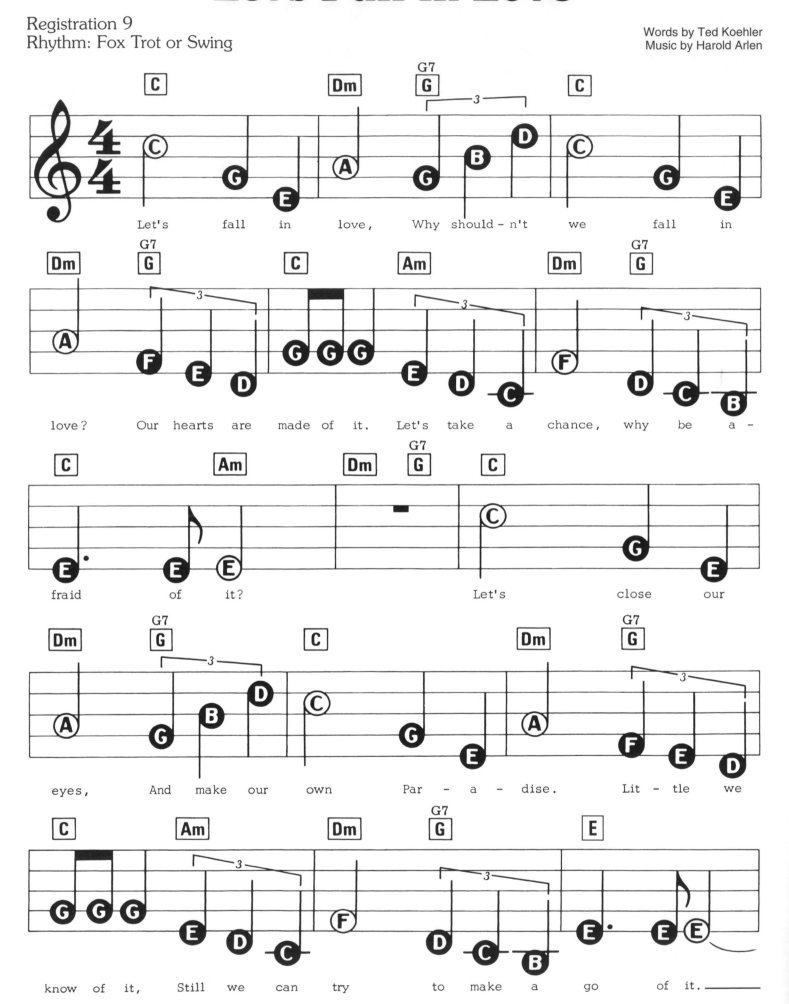

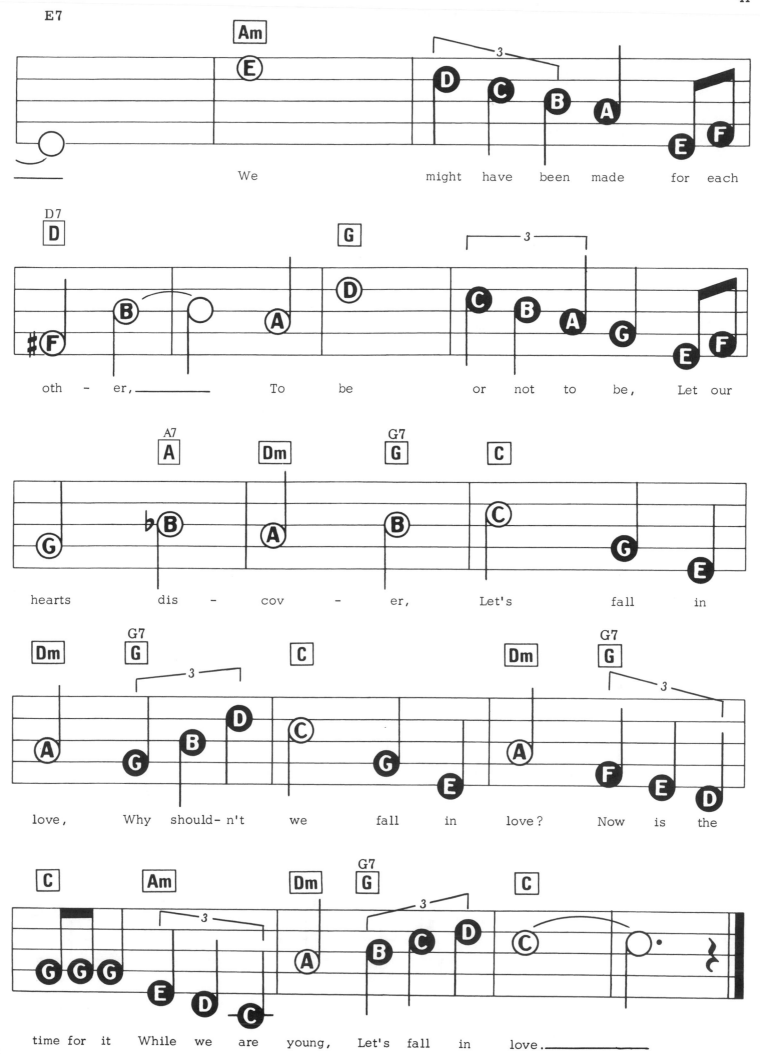

Lullaby of the Leaves

Registration 10
Rhythm: Fox Trot or Swing

Words by Joe Young
Music by Bernice Petkere

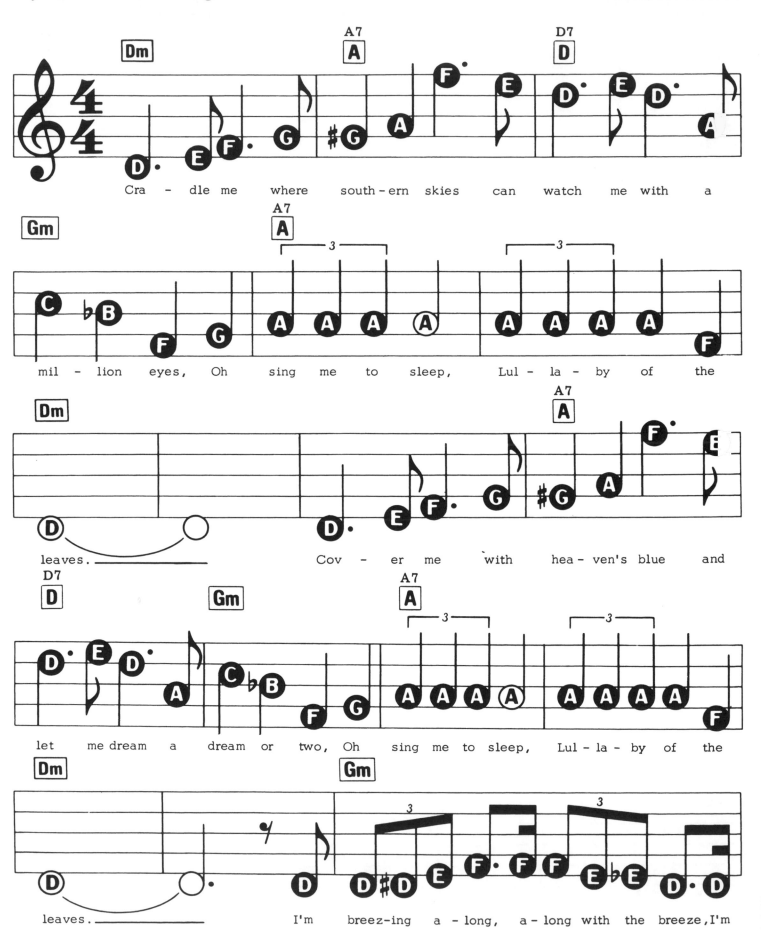

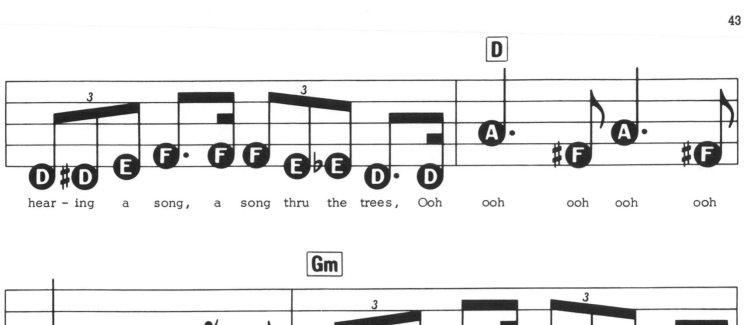

hear - ing a song, a song thru the trees, Ooh ooh ooh ooh ooh

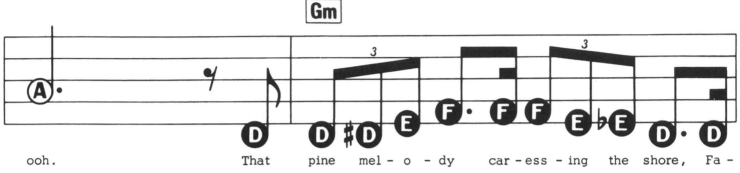

ooh. That pine mel - o - dy car - ess - ing the shore, Fa -

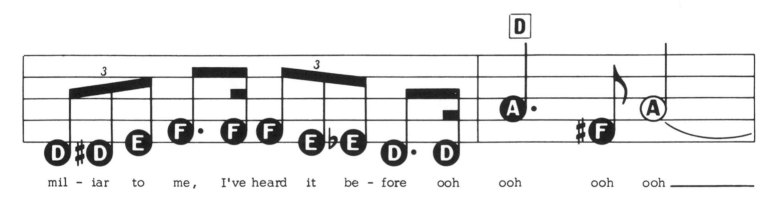

mil - iar to me, I've heard it be - fore ooh ooh ooh ooh

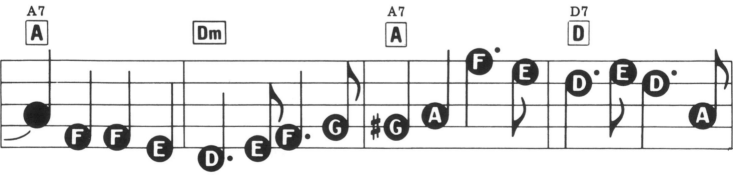

That's south - land, don't I feel it in my soul, and don't I know I've

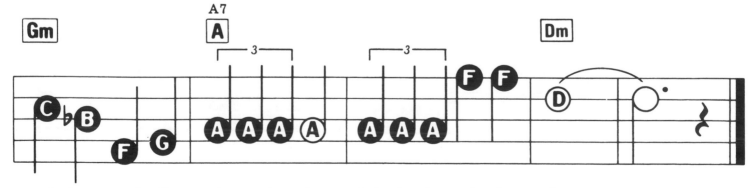

reached my goal, Oh sing me to sleep, Lul - la - by of the leaves.

Makin' Whoopee!
from WHOOPEE!

Registration 9
Rhythm: Fox Trot or Swing

Lyrics by Gus Kahn
Music by Walter Donaldson

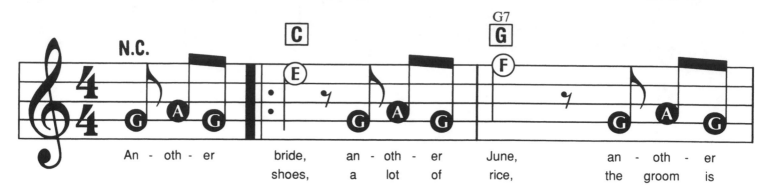

An - oth - er bride, an - oth - er June, an - oth - er
shoes, a lot of rice, the groom is

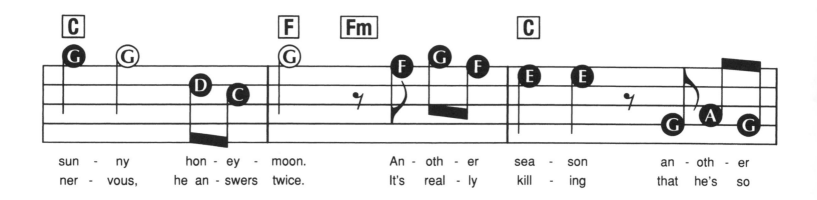

sun - ny hon - ey - moon. An - oth - er sea - son an - oth - er
ner - vous, he an - swers twice. It's real - ly kill - ing that he's so

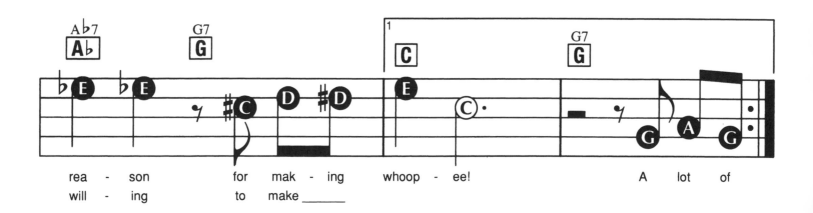

rea - son for mak - ing whoop - ee! A lot of
will - ing to make _____

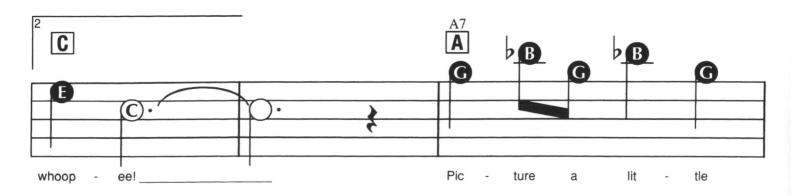

whoop - ee! _____ Pic - ture a lit - tle

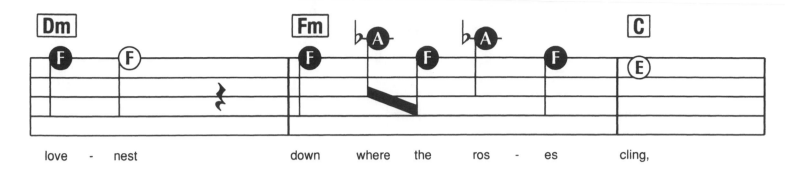

love - nest down where the ros - es cling,

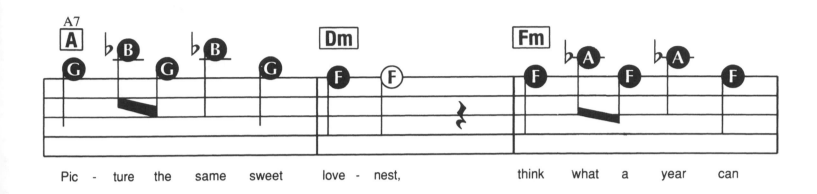

Pic - ture the same sweet love - nest, think what a year can

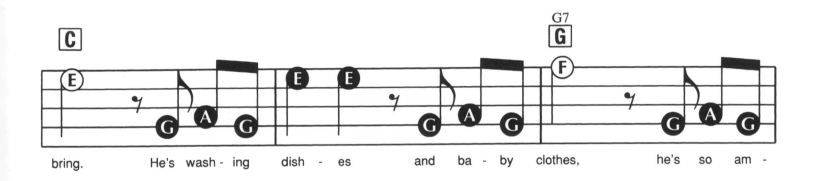

bring. He's wash - ing dish - es and ba - by clothes, he's so am -

bi - tious he e - ven sews. But don't for - get folks, that's what you

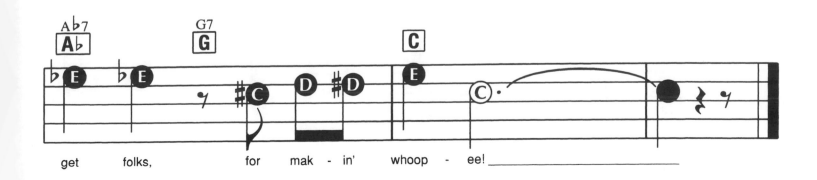

get folks, for mak - in' whoop - ee! _____

Pick Yourself Up
from SWING TIME

Registration 4
Rhythm: Fox Trot or Swing

Words by Dorothy Fields
Music by Jerome Kern

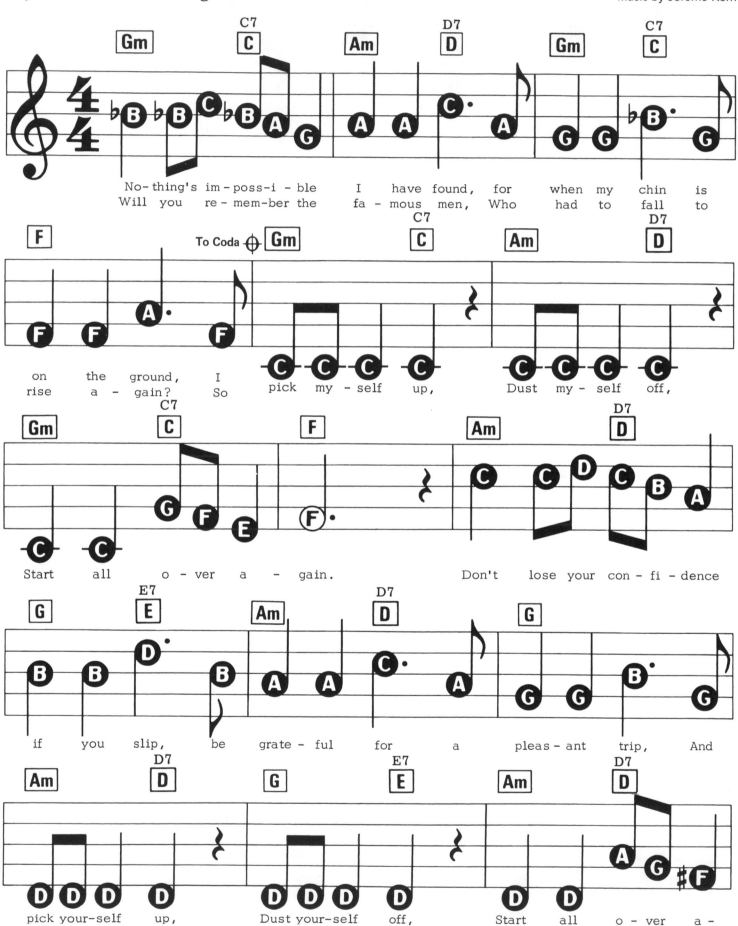

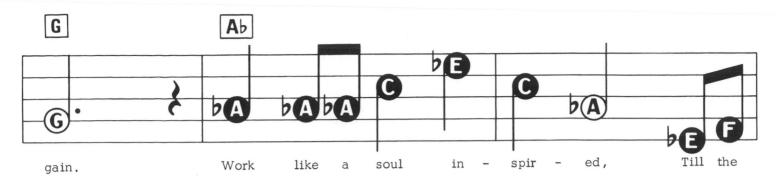

gain.   Work   like   a   soul   in - spir - ed,   Till the

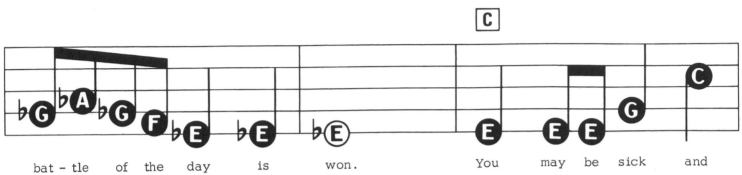

bat - tle   of   the   day   is   won.   You   may   be   sick   and

D.C. al Coda
(Return to beginning
Play to ⊕ and skip to Coda)

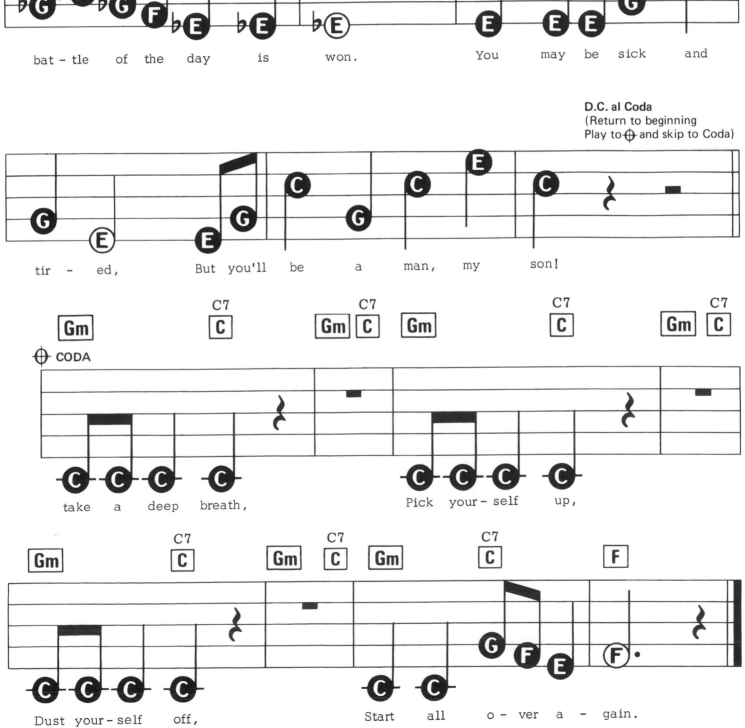

tir - ed,   But   you'll   be   a   man,   my   son!

take   a   deep   breath,   Pick   your - self   up,

Dust   your - self   off,   Start   all   o - ver   a - gain.

Same Old Saturday Night

Registration 2
Rhythm: Swing

Words by Sammy Cahn
Music by Frank Reardon

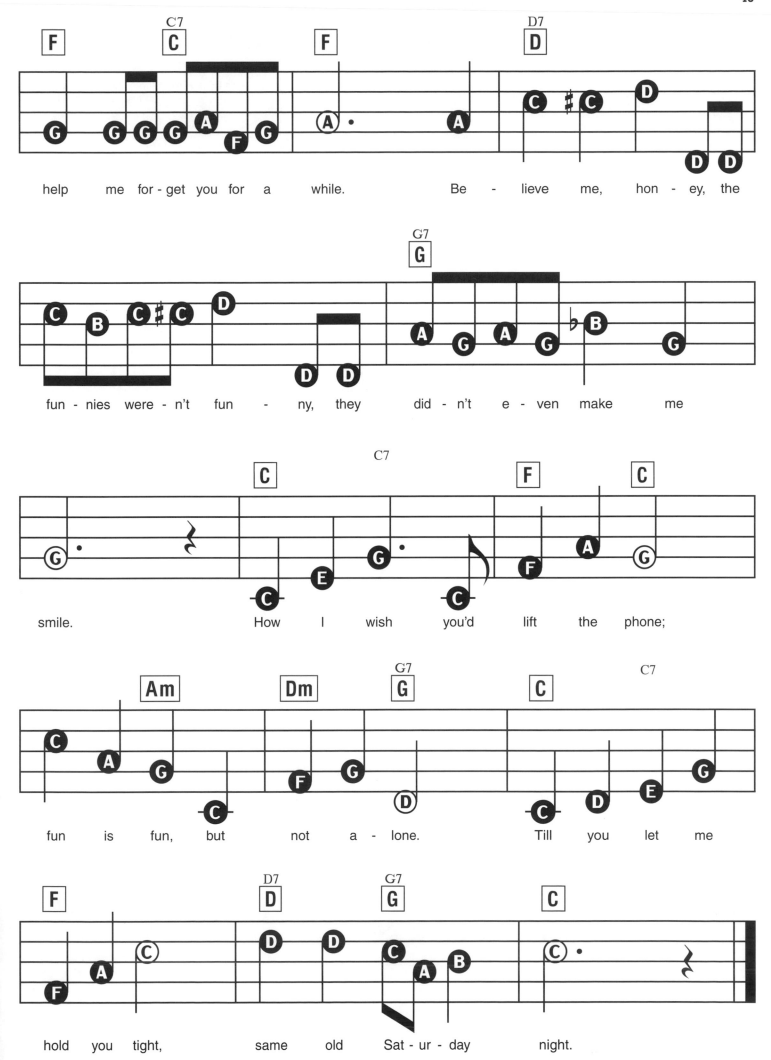

Satin Doll
from SOPHISTICATED LADIES

Registration 4
Rhythm: Swing or Jazz

Words by Johnny Mercer and Billy Strayhorn
Music by Duke Ellington

51

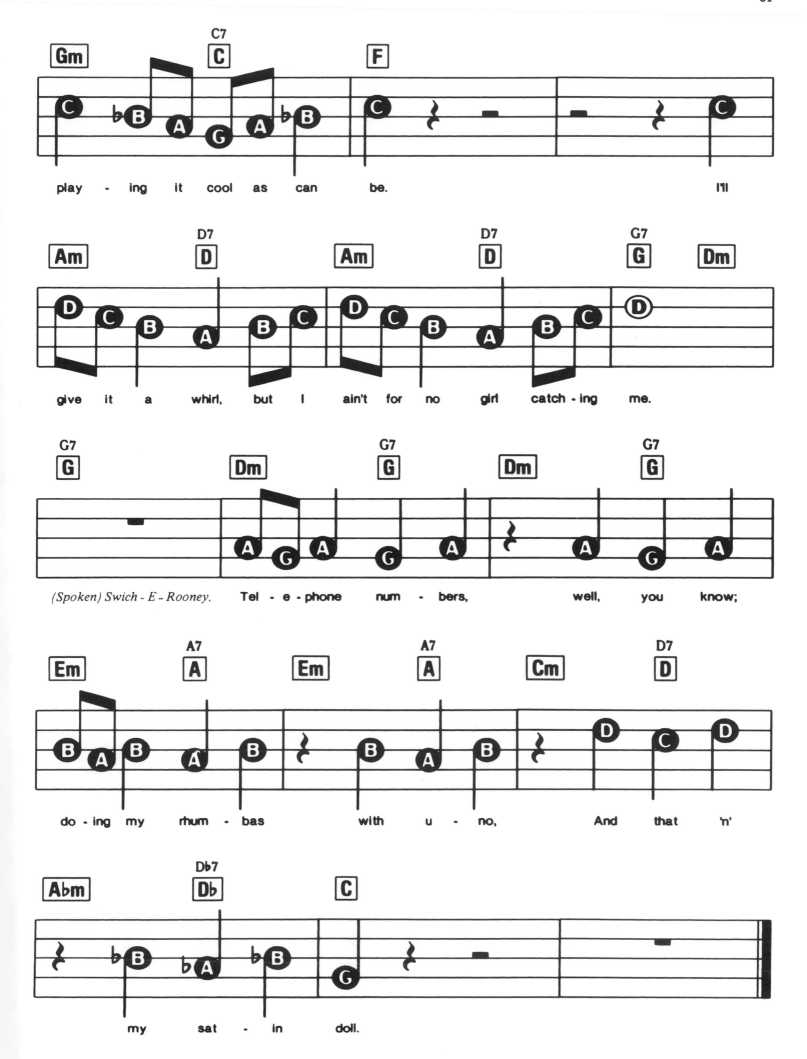

Sentimental Journey

Registration 2
Rhythm: Fox Trot or Swing

Words and Music by Bud Green,
Les Brown and Ben Homer

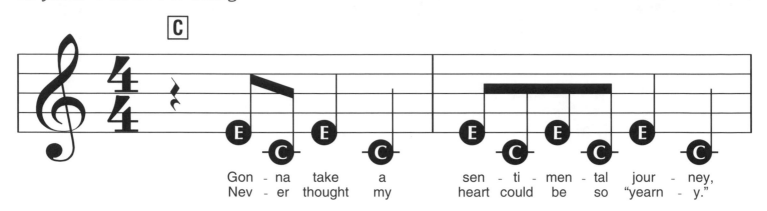

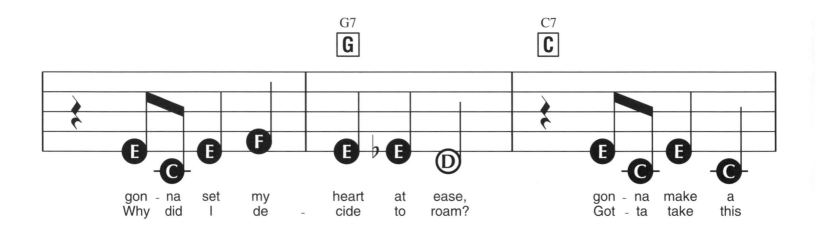

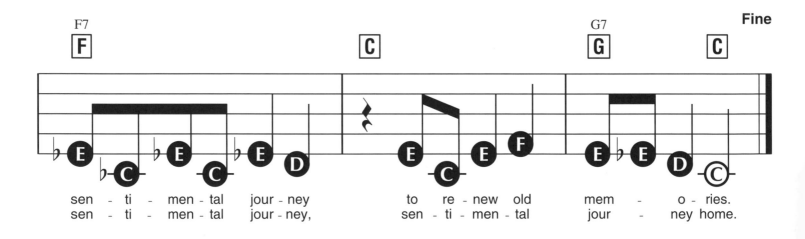

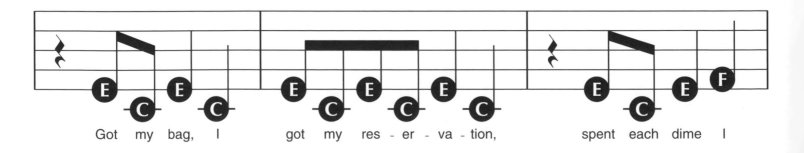

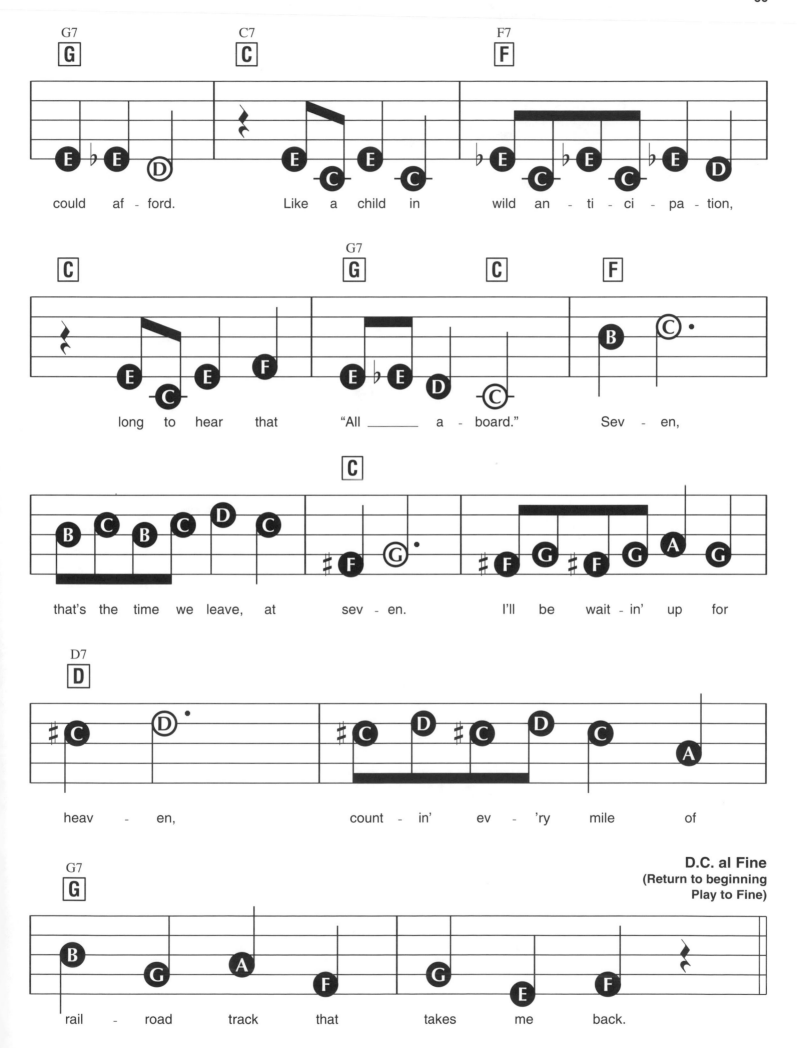

Stompin' at the Savoy

Registration 2
Rhythm: Swing

Words and Music by Benny Goodman,
Edgar Sampson, Chick Webb and Andy Razaf

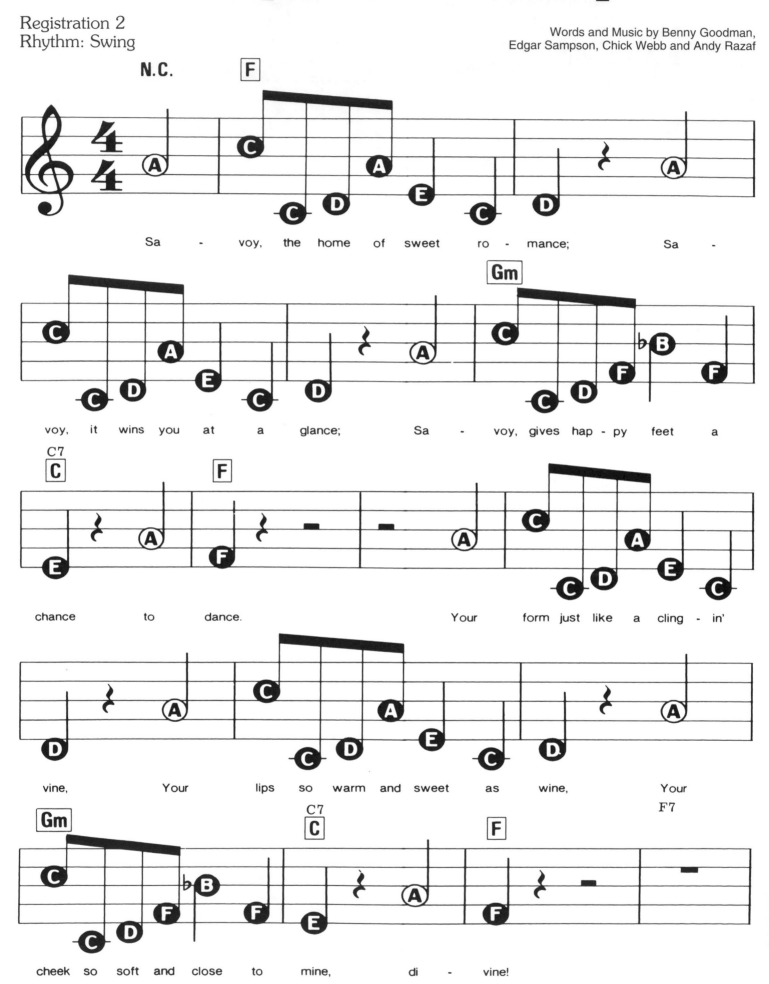

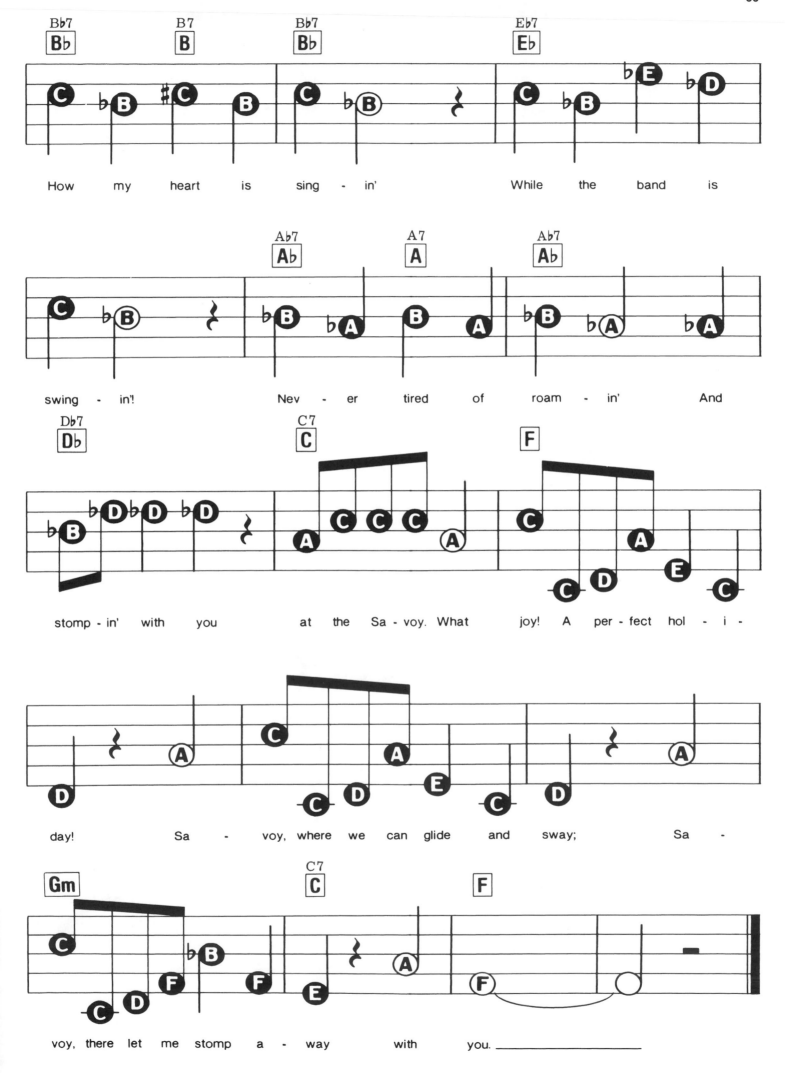

Swinging on a Star
from GOING MY WAY

Registration 2
Rhythm: Swing

Words by Johnny Burke
Music by Jimmy Van Heusen

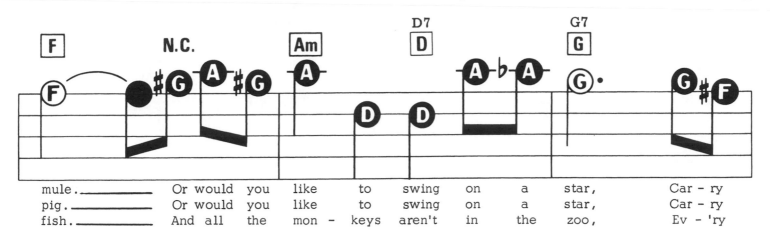

mule._____ Or would you like to swing on a star, Car - ry
pig._____ Or would you like to swing on a star, Car - ry
fish._____ And all the mon - keys aren't in the zoo, Ev - 'ry

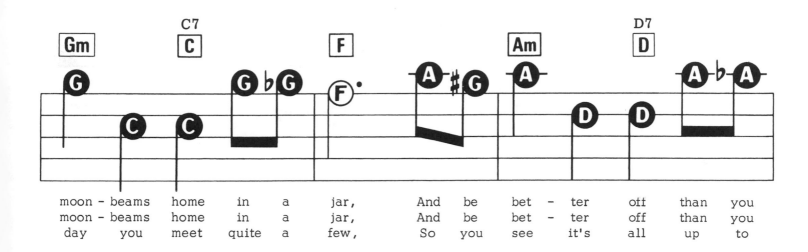

moon - beams home in a jar, And be bet - ter off than you
moon - beams home in a jar, And be bet - ter off than you
day you meet quite a few, So you see it's all up to

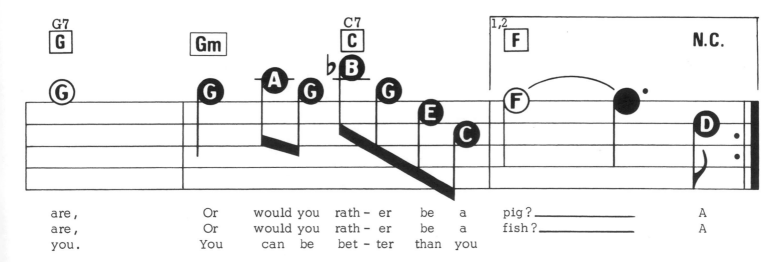

are, Or would you rath - er be a pig?_____ A
are, Or would you rath - er be a fish?_____ A
you. You can be bet - ter than you

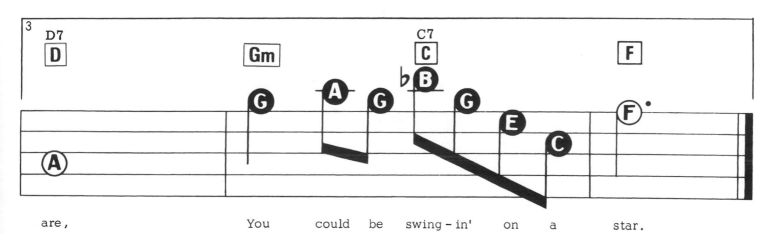

are, You could be swing-in' on a star.

Tuxedo Junction

Registration 1
Rhythm: Fox Trot or Swing

Words by Buddy Feyne
Music by Erskine Hawkins,
William Johnson and Julian Dash

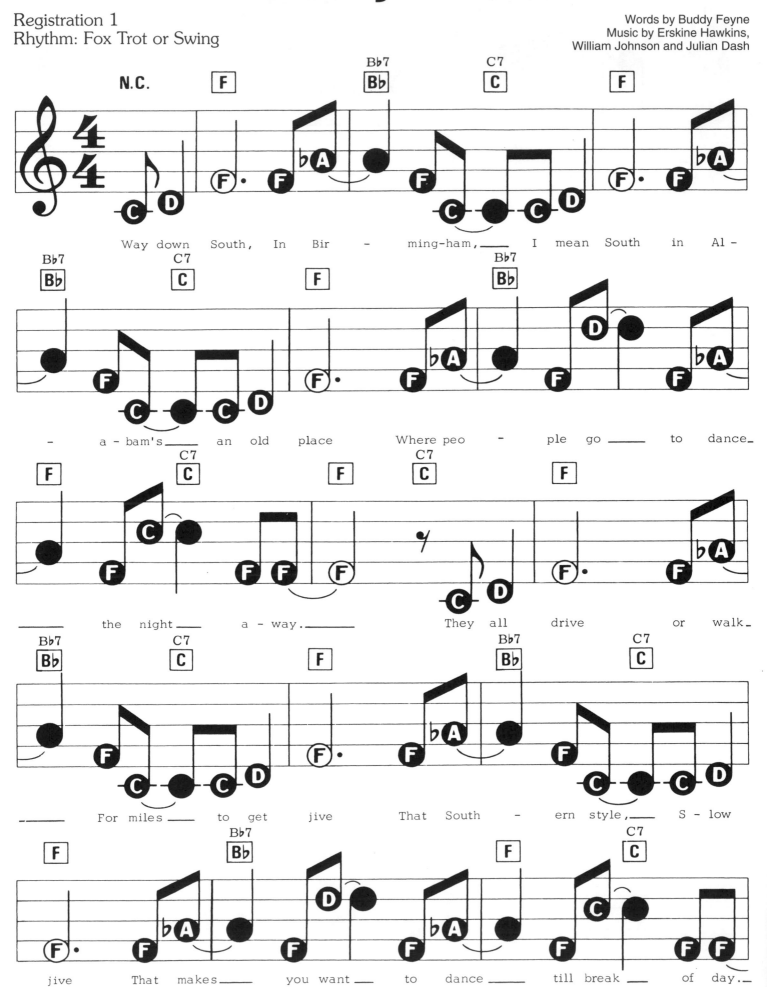

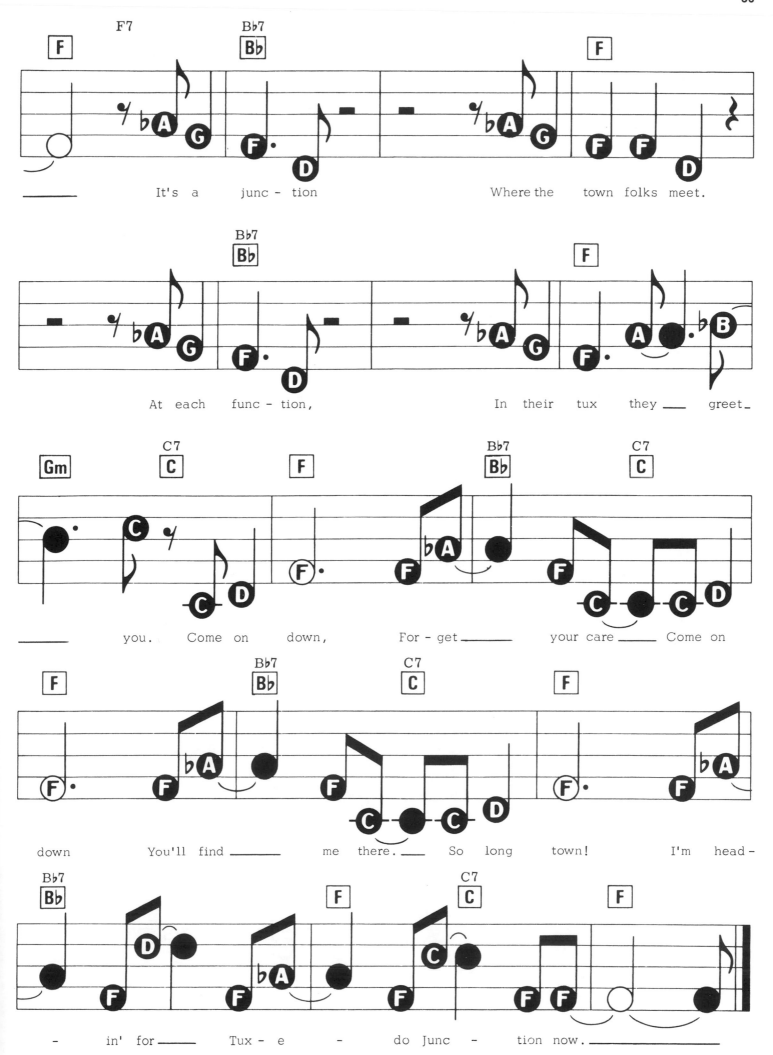

Witchcraft

Registration 9
Rhythm: Swing

Music by Cy Coleman
Lyrics by Carolyn Leigh

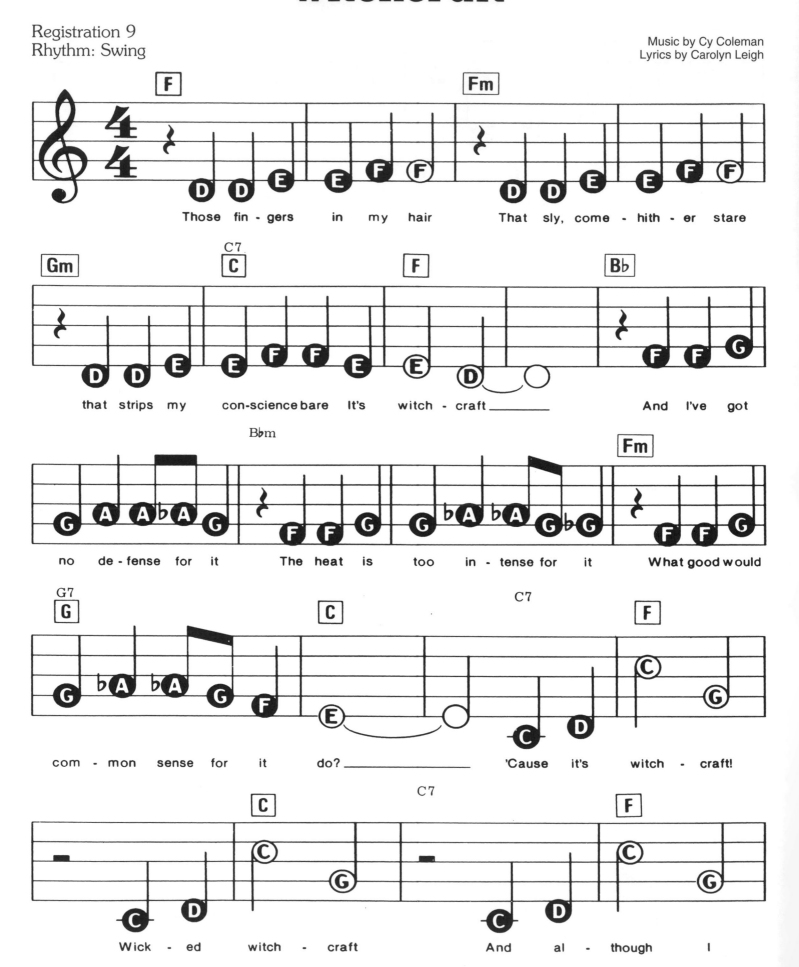

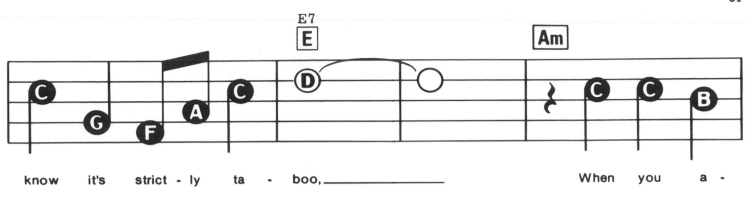

know it's strict-ly ta - boo,_____ When you a -

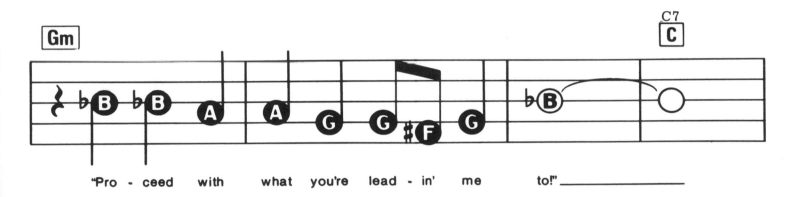

rouse the need in me, my heart says, "Yes, in - deed" in me,

"Pro - ceed with what you're lead - in' me to!"_____

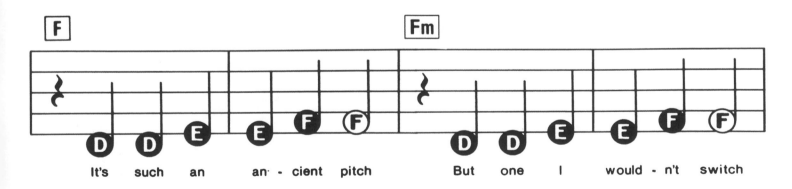

It's such an an - cient pitch But one I would - n't switch

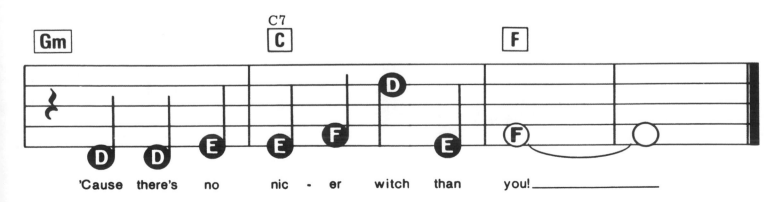

'Cause there's no nic - er witch than you!_____

You Came a Long Way
from St. Louis

Registration 7
Rhythm: Swing

Words by Bob Russell
Music by John Benson Brooks

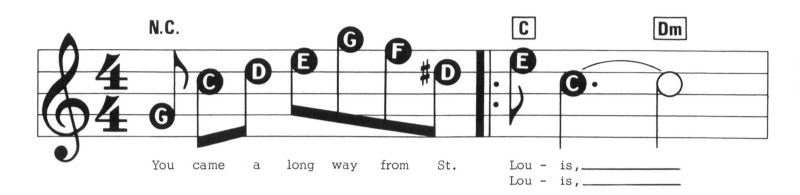

You came a long way from St. Lou - is,_____
Lou - is,_____

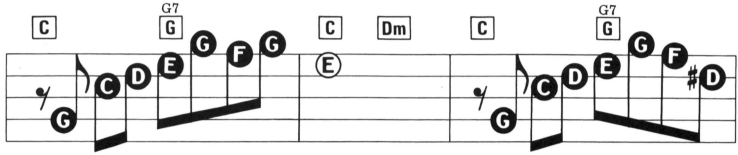

You climbed the lad - der of suc - cess.
You broke a 'lot - ta' hearts be - tween.
I've seen the Town And Coun-try
I've met a gang of gloom-y

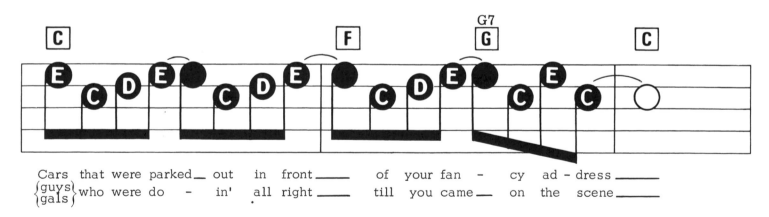

Cars that were parked__ out in front_____ of your fan - cy ad - dress_____
{guys}
{gals} who were do - in' all right_____ till you came__ on the scene_____

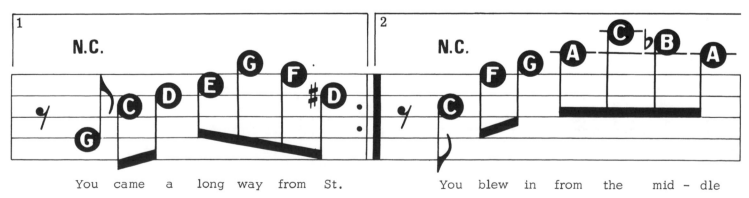

You came a long way from St.
You blew in from the mid - dle

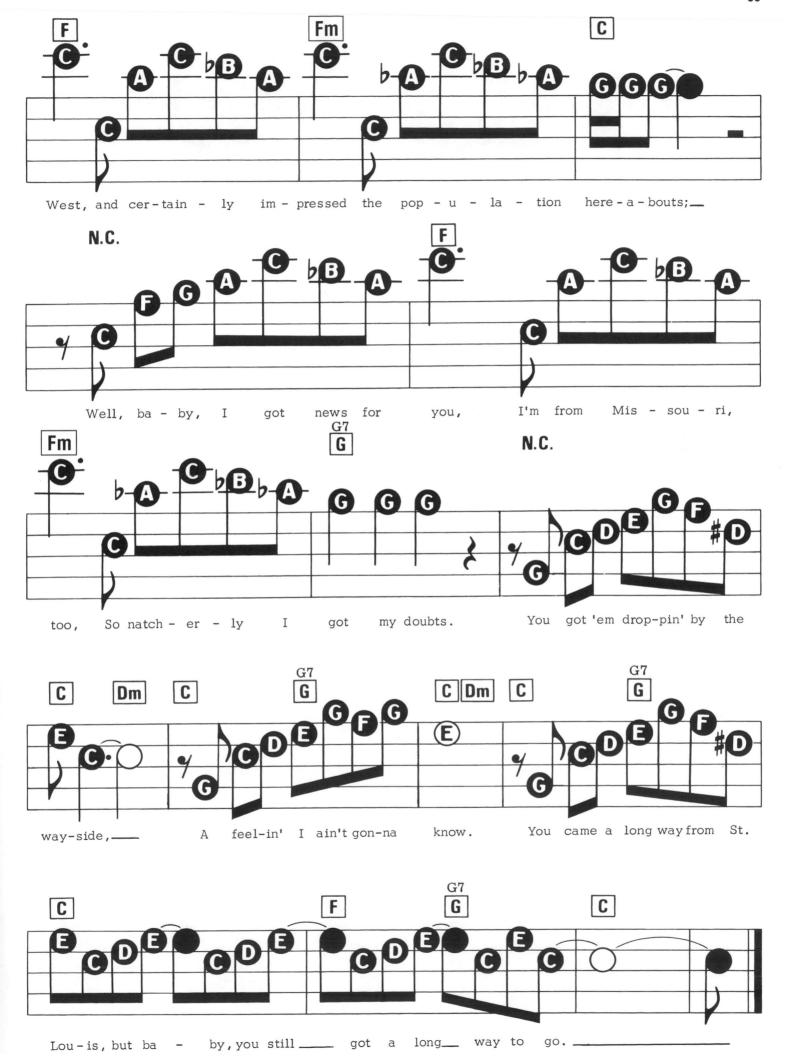

Registration Guide

- Match the Registration number on the song to the corresponding numbered category below. Select and activate an instrumental sound available on your instrument.

- Choose an automatic rhythm appropriate to the mood and style of the song. (Consult your Owner's Guide for proper operation of automatic rhythm features.)

- Adjust the tempo and volume controls to comfortable settings.

Registration

1	Mellow	Flutes, Clarinet, Oboe, Flugel Horn, Trombone, French Horn, Organ Flutes
2	Ensemble	Brass Section, Sax Section, Wind Ensemble, Full Organ, Theater Organ
3	Strings	Violin, Viola, Cello, Fiddle, String Ensemble, Pizzicato, Organ Strings
4	Guitars	Acoustic/Electric Guitars, Banjo, Mandolin, Dulcimer, Ukulele, Hawaiian Guitar
5	Mallets	Vibraphone, Marimba, Xylophone, Steel Drums, Bells, Celesta, Chimes
6	Liturgical	Pipe Organ, Hand Bells, Vocal Ensemble, Choir, Organ Flutes
7	Bright	Saxophones, Trumpet, Mute Trumpet, Synth Leads, Jazz/Gospel Organs
8	Piano	Piano, Electric Piano, Honky Tonk Piano, Harpsichord, Clavi
9	Novelty	Melodic Percussion, Wah Trumpet, Synth, Whistle, Kazoo, Perc. Organ
10	Bellows	Accordion, French Accordion, Mussette, Harmonica, Pump Organ, Bagpipes